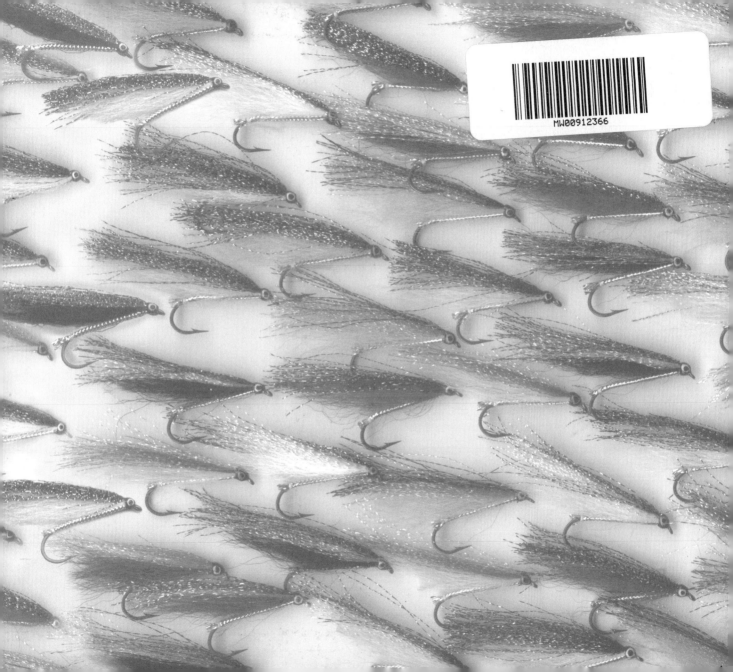

Fumbling with a Flyrod

Happy Birthday to John DAVID
on your 30th birthday

Patsi & Bob.

IAN COLIN JAMES

Fumbling with a Flyrod

Stories from the River

HarperCollins*Publishers*Ltd

FUMBLING WITH A FLYROD:
STORIES FROM THE RIVER
Copyright © 2000 by Ian Colin James.

http://www.harpercanada.com

HarperCollins books may be purchased for educational, business,
or sales promotional use. For information please write:
Special Markets Department, HarperCollins Canada,
55 Avenue Road, Suite 2900, Toronto, Ontario,
Canada M5R 3L2.

First HarperCollins hardcover ed. ISBN 0-00-200042-3
First HarperCollins trade paper ed. ISBN 0-00-638539-7

Canadian Cataloguing in Publication Data

James, Ian Colin, 1960–
    Fumbling with a flyrod: stories from the river

ISBN 0-00-200042-3
    1. Fly fishing—Anecdotes.
    I. Title.

SH456.J35 2000   799.1'24   C99-932142-0

00 01 02 03 04 RRD 6 5 4 3 2 1

Printed and bound in the United States

Cover Fly: The Murray
Tied by: Ian Colin James
Photograph: Ian Colin James

Endpapers: A school of Winkies
Tied by: Ian Colin James
Layout & design: Evan Frith, Roy Nicol & Ian Colin James

Dedication

To my ancestors and all those who have gone before,
and for Alexander and those who will follow.

CONTENTS

Fumbling with a Flyrod

Perfect Conditions

So, Ian, we'll try below the sewage plant. Like I said, I've never fished downstream from it, but it looks okay. I fished above the plant once last summer. It's all riffle-pool-riffle-pool water. Lots of 6- and 7-inchers, but nothing big."

"Plus, Les, if you need to be back at twelve to spend time with the wife and kiddy, it's only fifteen minutes away, so we won't have to drive all over hell's half-acre to get there. We might as well try it. Could be full of 20-inch smallmouth and we'll never know until we go. With your jigs and my flies, we'll have all the bases covered. What time do you want to go?"

"Early."

"How early, Les? It's almost light at six." With hardly a pause he replied, "Five-thirty."

"My stuff'll be at the end of the driveway. And,

Les, try not to run over any skunks on the way over, will ya? The neighbors are still looking at the rubber marks from the last time. See ya."

"See ya then," he said, just before I hung up the phone.

Our last time was a five o' clock start. I was sitting on the front steps at the house, finishing a coffee, waiting for Les, listening to the birds working through some voice exercises and scales as they warmed up for the dawn chorus. A big, fluffy skunk—large enough for a throw rug—was rooting for grubs in the front lawn. He'd wandered around the side of the house, looked at me, toddled down the driveway, sniffed at the pile of fishing gear, then set about turfing the turf. I don't spray the lawn, preferring to let the birds and the local wildlife use the garden as an all-you-can-eat buffet. Plus, all that chemical junk eventually ends up in the waterways, and that can't be good. The skunk was digging up more divots than a rookie on a golf course. In a three-dimensional and fully mobile state, as opposed to the flat and stiff highway condition, skunks are characters and good clean family entertainment. Viewer discretion is never advised unless they are setting about the neighbor's garbage. Then again—it's not the skunk who is responsible for the PG rating; it's the antics of the angry human who just can't seem to get it right. Sort of like: Don't blame the porcupines for chewing and devouring the wooden deck at the cottage because someone was peeing on it. As Jack Nicholson said in *As Good as It Gets*, "Why can't we all just get along?"

Even in the busiest of Canadian cities, there is not much going on at five in the morning—it's the time of the day reserved for garbage pickups, newspaper deliveries and criminal activity—and you can hear traffic from several blocks away. Les was no exception, and I heard him coming long before he arrived. The skunk did, too, and started heading for the road—I said they were characters, I didn't

say they were particularly smart characters—and I knew what was going to happen. Les, who would be looking for the house, might not see "the wee fella" heading onto the road. To get to the end of the driveway and warn Les, I'd have to pass the skunk, so that was not an option. The car came around the corner, and its lights lit up the skunk. It froze, doing the "deer in the headlights" thing. Les hit the lights, hit the brakes and hit the horn. The rubber hit the road, the neighborhood hit the bedroom light switches and the skunk hit the trail. Needless to say, my early-morning fishing trips were the hot topic for several days.

There are very few folk I would fish with, just for the sheer pleasure of being outside, having a hoot and a holler, and freely exchanging fishing ideas—knowing the information will go no further. Les is one of those folk. He's a master at catching smallmouth bass, possessed (with angling knowledge) and is one of the few folk who—*on a hunch*—I'd get out of bed at five o' clock, or earlier, to accompany to a fishing spot I'd never tried before. He is the only fisherman I know who has battled it out with a beaver in a tug-of-war, over a branch he'd snagged into. The beaver won, but Les put up a hell of a fight and before the hook finally pulled free, leaving the beaver to swim off with its prize, he almost landed the buck-toothed rodent twice. I'd have paid good money to see him try to lip-land that!

Les has only one failing: he carries a curse. It's nothing too serious, but those who fish with him have all been struck with some type of angling misfortune. When I started hanging out with the lads at the Thames River Anglers Association, I was warned not to fish with Les on the Maitland River as this seems to be the epicenter of his bad karma. I've only done it once. One snowy spring morning he called, complaining that no one would go fishing with him there. We both knew the steelhead were in, so I succumbed to the temptation on the condition that we were never to be within casting distance of each other. On his last excursion, the wind drove a lure Les was casting into the back of the skull of his angling companion. Les had just busted the lure out of its package and sharpened the hooks. The lure never made it to the water. The hooks were embedded so deeply in his skull that the emergency department at the local hospital, which deals with numerous cases on a yearly basis, had to call in a specialist to get the hooks out. The highlight of *my* trip was slipping off some pack ice into water that stopped inches short of the top of my waders. I took this to be an omen, so on the way home I informed him that this was the last time we'd be fishing the Maitland together.

At four a.m., some eight hours after I'd hung up the phone with Les, I stopped working on the manuscript for this book, finished off a slice of watermelon dusted with cinnamon, then toddled off to bed. At five, the alarm went off. By five-twenty, I'd showered using a nonperfumed soap—perfume attracts biting bugs—and finished off some stir-fried chicken and veggies, leftovers that were trying to hide on the lowest shelf of the fridge. Then I guzzled down a couple of pints of water to prehydrate myself for the upcoming adventure—fishing with Les is *always* an adventure—and headed out the door into the gray, muggy twilight.

At five-twenty-five I was in the driveway, digging through the many varied and wonderful contents of my car trunk, trying to decide if I should take my 35mm Canon T-70 on the trip, while basting myself with sunscreen. There is something "just not right" about putting sunscreen on in the dark. The camera has great sentimental value, so I wanted to look out for its well-being, and my not taking it would ensure that Les and I would catch something big or something weird. My concerns about taking it were twofold: one, it felt like it was going to rain, something *serious*, not just a good soaker; and, two, it's not wise to be wading with a camera in uncharted territory. In July, floating downriver for a couple of hundred yards, looking for an exit point, is no big deal. Floating downriver, trying to hang onto your fishing gear while trying to keep a camera above the water, *is*.

I had just fished my tackle out from the back of the car when Les rolled to a stop across the end of the driveway, parking under a streetlight. I knew it was five-thirty. We shook hands, exchanging whispered greetings. "Think I should bring my camera or should I leave it in the trunk until I get back? I'd like to get a few pike, gar pike or pickerel shots for the book."

"Don't know. Feels like it's gonna rain, and we've never fished here before, so it might be kinda tricky." Although we both knew he didn't have to, he added, "If you don't take it, we have a better chance of getting something big. At this time of the year, any pike in there will be an incidental catch; there's not enough numbers of them to target them specifically. Haven't heard of anyone getting a gar out of there, but I suppose they could be up that far. The pickerel should be long gone, but I did get a 5-pounder out of here this time last year. If you bring a camera we probably won't get anything big."

"True enough, Les. True enough." All anglers who are lucky enough to be able to spend many hours on the water know that a camera is the kiss of death to an angling trip. Quite often, when I do take a camera into a river, I will say things to my fishing buddies or clients in a very loud voice, but not loud enough to arouse fishy suspicions: "Wish I'd brought a camera" or "Too bad I left the photography stuff in the car." The camera is always slung behind my back, just to make sure the fish can't see it. If anybody other than Les were to tell me they took a pickerel out of this river, or any other river, five months after their spring spawning run, I'd have a very hard time believing it. With Les, however, it was just another day at the office.

He was picking up my rod and waders, and heading to his car, as I stored the camera safely away in the trunk and rechecked my bag for terminal tackle. Hook-file; spare hook-file; three spools of line for leaders—4-, 6- and 8-pound; license; cash for coffee on the way there; needle-nose pliers; four empty 35mm film canisters full of split shot; my 1 1/2 inch tall, plastic but lucky Elmer Fudd, complete with carrots stuck in the end of his shotgun; and two boxes of flies. All

present and correct. "Les, watch the rod. I just pulled it from the trunk, so it's still got a leader and a fly attached to it from my trip yesterday. Watch the hook, it's awfully sharp."

"I'll put your pole in between the front seats so it won't get all tangled up with my junk back there in the trunk," he replied.

"Thanks," I said, instinctively checking for the keys in my back pocket before I closed the trunk to my car, then started walking down the driveway. He held my rod up to the streetlight, inspecting the leader. "You still running straight Fire Line?" He opened the back right door, slipped the rod in between the front seats and closed the door.

"Absolutely. I've used it to skip 8-pound carp over the surface, and Stephan landed that 35-pound hen chinook salmon last fall on straight six. Plus I'd feel as guilty as hell if I didn't, since I was the first guy to use it for leader material after I got a box of pre-production spools in 1995. My bite detection has gone through the roof, and the fish can't wear it out running it over rocks. Can't beat it. The stuff works, why change?"

"Think the unwashed masses will ever catch on to using it?"

"Nah! They haven't for the past four years. It doesn't have a fly fisherman on the pack, and it doesn't have any of those slick, leader-material names on it, so they'll probably miss it. Everyone's on the super-thin, ultra-clear bandwagon at the moment. Something else will soon be the flavor of the month."

"Well, I guess if it ain't broke" were the last words he said, before he slipped behind the wheel. "Don't fix it." I finished his sentence, closed his trunk and wandered around to the passenger side.

Two coffees and a muffin found their way in through the driver's window at the donut-shop drive-thru. Les checked the markings on the lids to make sure we got the right ones, then he pulled out onto the deserted and very quiet street, heading out of town, toward the sewage plant and the inevitable sunrise. "How's the book going?" he asked

"Not bad. It's tougher than I thought. The good thing is that by hanging out with the boys at the club I've got enough material for a dozen books."

"Yeah. Great fishermen, but they're plagued by bad luck."

"I'm having a hard time trying to let folks know how attached you get to your fishing poles. They get to be your little buddies, make you feel confident and secure—sort of like some women with their handbags."

"Yeah. That little ultra-lite of mine in the trunk is about ten years old. I've never seen you use anything other than that fly pole for bass. How old is it?"

"About fifteen years. I only use it for small-mouth, it's got a great backbone. They don't make 'em anymore." I pulled the top off the muffin, took a big bite and looked out at the shop windows. Les was switching gears. "JEEZUS!" he shouted, simultaneously slamming on the brakes. My head shot forward, the seatbelt tightened up, then, as I rebounded into the back of the seat, hot coffee spilled and splashed onto my leg. Almost choking on the mouthful of muffin, I couldn't speak, but gave him a wide-eyed, worried look, *exactly* the same as the one he was giving me. There was a loud crack, just before Les, with eyes as big as saucers said, "I think I just busted your pole." "Wh-a-ffa-fa-faa," I forced down the mouthful of muffin, and as soon as I was past the point of choking, said, "What?"

"I think I bumped it changing gears or I sat on it or something."

I took another large swallow. "What?"

He turned to look at the back seat, saying, "Open the back door." I hadn't a clue what he was going on about, but when I heard the words "back door" in conjunction with "fishing pole," "Uh–oh!" sprang to mind. Confused at the goings-on, I open the door, but I still had no clue what had happened. What I *was* processing was not good. A man I'd never seen panic or get flustered, except in the company of large spiders, was becoming frantic in the front seat; we were parked in the middle of the street; and he was telling me to open the back door. Fearing the worst, I reached around and opened the door. "The pole's busted," he said. I closed the door and we headed off down the street. "Jeesuz, Ian, I don't know

how that happened. I must have bumped it changing gears or something. I'm sorry."

"No worries," I said, "It's only a flyrod and nobody got hurt." I looked at him, then added, "Yet!"

"We're only five minutes from your house. Want me to go back so you can get another pole?"

"Nah! I'll wait till we're done. When we get back, I'll lay all my rods on the driveway so you can back over them and get them all at once. No point in spending the rest of the season popping them off one at a time." We chuckled and turned the conversation to making fun of the advertising in the shop windows along the street, both agreeing, but failing to understand, why most folk must sleep late on Saturday mornings.

We pulled into the sewage-plant parking lot, just as the warm glow from the sun was illuminating the chain-link fence surrounding the facility. Stepping out onto the dusty gravel parking lot, we had a good stretch, limbering up for what was about to take place. The sky was a solid gray mass, and we both had the feeling it was getting ready to deliver something really nasty. The trees and plants framing the parking lot were limp, and the grass was dry and crunchy.

A few eastern kingbirds, hard to miss due to their black and white penguin-like markings, were sitting on top of the fence, using it as a launching pad for picking off insects. At 8 inches tall, these birds are very conspicuous, and they're well known for their aerobatics when catching insects or plucking berries from bushes. These aviators pack an attitude. Whenever I've watched a hawk, owl or a crow being harassed or chased across the treetops by a pack of smaller birds, there's usually a kingbird up there in the mob, "putting in the boot."

I slipped my car keys and loose change under the rubber floor mat, then we went around to the back passenger door to survey the damage to the rod.

The leader was missing and so was the top 6 inches of the rod. A thorough check of the back seat did not produce the leader, the fly or the missing rod part. It was starting to take on a supernatural aura, then the lightbulb went on. Les had put the rod between the seats *inside* the car, but the fly and leader were left dangling on the *outside* when he closed the back door. As we merrily drove along, the fly—we assumed—had bumped into the spinning tire or it had snagged the wheel hub, ripping the leader off. Something had to give, and that something was the tip of the rod. When I opened the door, the missing chunk dropped out onto the street. Les looked at me, saying, "Next time I put your gear into the car, I'll make sure that I put *all of it* inside." We took a pair of line clippers, trimmed the busted section down to the next guide, got our gear together and, with Les leading the way, headed down a bike path toward the river.

Just before we got to the treeline, and the thickets of stinging nettles and tall grasses fringed with waves of Queen Anne's lace, Les poked his rod out in front of himself and, as he walked, began sweeping it up and down. I gave him a puzzled look. "I'm de-spidering," he said.

"Ho."

"Those big black and yellow ones freak me out,

the ones with the zigzag pattern in the middle of the web."

"I know, the black-and-yellow Argiope. Vicious as hell. I got nailed by one crossing over the island in the Saugeen three years ago. It fell down the inside of my shirt sleeve and, when I moved my arm—whammo! They pack quite the punch. My arm was black and blue for days. July and August are the months for those big black and yellow beasties. Les, I've seen them with a body an inch and a quarter long and almost as fat as a peach stone, with their webs so thick in the grass along the trails of the riverbank that they looked like fog."

His spinning rod was wiggling up and down a little bit quicker. So I did the only decent thing I could, and continued on. "It's a large-scale operation, capable of bringing down a dragonfly or, by the looks of things, small birds, mammals and unsuspecting livestock. Those lads probably ate Eensy-Weensy and have never had the need to climb up a waterspout." He was now de-spidering with renewed vigor.

"You know, Les, when I was a kid, I was kind of afraid of spiders. My granda said I was being silly, so I went to his woodpile and trapped a big fat garden spider in a jam jar. I took the lid off and tipped the jar upside down on my head. The spider moved around on my hair, then crawled down my face. Ever since then, I've never been afraid of them, but I do have a healthy respect for those big ones. Boy, this looks like heavy-duty spider country. There's gotta be hundreds concealed in this thick cover."

Les had picked up the pace, and his anxious rod sweeps were getting faster. We pushed though the drifts of 5-foot-tall stinging nettles, clumps of brambles and chest-high grasses until, fifteen minutes later, drenched in sweat, we popped out from under the tree canopy onto the expanse of the river.

Here the water flow is controlled by a series of dams, so there is no floodplain. The vegetation on the bank ends and the river begins. There is an intimate, almost claustrophobic, feel to fishing these types of locations, where the big-sky feeling of a floodplain is gone.

Apart from our heavy breathing, there was precious little noise, except for the distant gurgling of the riffles further upstream. Both banks were a solid mass of trees, dark green walls towering up to the gray ceiling of clouds. The sun was just hitting the tops of the trees on the far bank, some 60 yards away, and everything else was still trapped in the dour morning twilight. A heavy air hung over the sanctity of the river. Highlighted by a stab of sunlight, the tops of the trees looked like stained-glass windows, giving the quiet scene cathedral-like qualities, where reverence and hushed tones were in order. Pockets of mist hung like incense between the shadows and the water.

There was hardly a ripple on the surface of the long placid pool spread out before us. In hushed tones—I was waiting for "Bless me Father, for I have sinned"—Les broke the silence. His muffled voice echoed but failed to reach the far bank. "The bubbles up there are from the plant outflow. I was hoping they used an ultra-violet system, but I don't think they do. Can you smell the chlorine?"

"Yeah."

"We'll not get much in here. The big fish don't like that stuff."

"Yeah," I said. "We should get some rock bass along the far edge. We're here anyway, so we best give it a shot. You never know. Looks like nice pike water."

An hour of fishing produced nothing more than a mess of rock bass and a bunch of 4- and 5-inch smallmouth . This was serious fishing, not the typical "let's go and have a good time" type of angling trip. There was no time to stop for a break, to take on water or to let out water. This was a reconnaissance mission, with our two primary objectives being to cover every inch of usable water and to put some impressive numbers of fish on the board. We had only about six hours to find out as much as we could about this section of water. Together we were a well-oiled fishing machine. Gone was the rhetoric of jig fisherman versus fly fisherman, and gone were the taunts and slags of how poorly the other person was doing. Numbers was the only name of the game. Our system was perfect. Using his heavy jigs, Les could get down into the deep runs and make longer casts into areas I could not hit with the flyrod. I, on the other hand, could fish shallow areas or brush piles and stumps, where getting busted off only meant the loss of a lump of fur and feathers, areas where Les definitely did not want to risk losing some of his more expensive terminal tackle. "Jeezus, Les, this is great-looking water and the conditions are perfect. We've got to get a couple of 18-inchers out of here."

"At least. This water's amazing; when we're out of the way of this chlorine, we should be into a ton of 2- and 3-pound fish."

"Any thoughts on numbers?"

"Well over a hundred, maybe one-fifty, but lots of the small 6-inchers."

"Yeah, I'm thinking around the one-twenty mark."

We'd racked up numbers like these on several occasions. Size, in these instances, did not matter. Everything counted, even the smaller 4-inch fish. It was an exercise in finding out how good the population base was, and scouting the area for spots that would hold larger fish. The better holding water would be fished more heavily at a later date, when we'd skipped over the Freeway Sections—areas of the river which could not sustain a population of bass, like slow muddy bottoms or water that was less than 6 inches deep—holding the smaller fish. On future big-fish trips, we'd cover a lot of river, 2 miles minimum, and hit very specific targets. We'd fish the spot, get out of the river, quickly walk down the bank to the next spot, fish it, and then the process would continue, leap-frogging past each other, methodically working downstream.

"Are you getting to the bottom? I can't get down with this fly. It's gotta be over 8 feet deep and I can't mend around those branches in the middle of the pool."

"Yeah, my jig is tapping out once in a while. Let's work our way down to the tail end of the pool. There's *gotta* be some bigger fish in here."

"Has to be. Bet they are sitting at the face of those big boulders, just before this slips into the riffles. You take a wander down there and have a go at the front of the rocks. I'm gonna tie on a Halloween Caddis, nip down below you, and try the riffles."

Les took two steps past me and threw out a long cast. His line tightened up. "There's something a bit bigger." His rod, bent over to the cork, arched in slow steady throbs. But the fish wasn't zipping around in the pool the way a bass would. Just in case, I reeled in my line and stepped out of the way onto the bank. The fish was now scooting around in the pool. He looked at me. "Might be a redhorse or a carp."

"Can't be. If it were either of them, you'd be spooled by now. I haven't a clue what you've got." Two minutes later, he was removing the jig from the mouth of a 3-pound pickerel. He held up the fish. "Shows you. You never know what you're gonna get till you try. You can either fish, or park your butt in front of the TV fishing shows and fake it. This fish has been in here for about six months and he ain't doing too well. Look how long and thin his body is compared to the head.

It's kind of anemic-looking." Kneeling down, he gently released the fish then added, "We'll need to keep this drift in mind for when the spring run is on next year."

The sun chased away the heavy cloud cover, and three hours of fishing put our total at just under a hundred fish. We'd covered a mile or so of water, and with the temperature in the mid-eighties, high humidity and not a breath of wind, it was very tough sledding. We'd fished some water that screamed out that it was holding fish—lots of big fish—but the biggest we'd hooked was a 15-inch smallmouth. I took it on the surface of a scum-covered back eddy. It was starting to become frustrating. Fishing new water for the first time is like an Easter egg hunt. You know they are hiding out there someplace and the trick is finding those hidey-holes. I love the challenge of fishing new water. It keeps me on my toes, and there is none of the complacency that comes from knowing which casts will produce fish. To be successful, you have to think; to stay upright, you have to stay alert.

Between us, over the years, Les and I had landed

thousands of bass, from spots that were atrocious compared with the stuff we'd been fishing over, but this was a stumper. Prime water, where you know there are two or three big fish lurking around, was producing nothing. Les turned and said, "Any ideas?"

"Nothing I haven't tried," I replied.

Wading downstream, we noticed the river hadn't been getting pounded by other anglers. There were no access points—therefore no garbage on the banks—and no piles of discarded line. The algae on the rocks around our feet was like a plush green carpet. In contrast, scuffed-up algae on the river bed would be a sure bet that the area was being heavily travelled and heavily fished. The lack of angling pressure compounded our frustrations. This was one less thing to use as an excuse for not catching larger fish.

We were heading down the center of the river, hitting likely looking spots. Les made a move to cross a particularly fast section. "I don't know. That looks kinda fast, and, if you go for a float, you'll get tangled up in that log jam downriver.

And, Les, I'll have a bitch of a time trying to get the car keys out of your vest when you're impaled on one of those busted branches." He paused, thought about the dangers, weighed up the consequences and changed his mind. As we studied the river, looking for a safe route, we exchanged "once-I-went-a-floating" horror stories.

He was winter steelheading, the only one on the river and it was well below freezing. The water was packed with fast-flowing slush, and there were several ice jams piled up in the center of the river. Realizing things looked far too dangerous to fish, he turned to leave, slipped off the bank and was instantly carried downstream by the current. Luckily, or so he thought, he hit a large chunk of ice—about 15 feet square—in the middle of the river and managed to scramble onto it, figuring that someone would eventually come by, see him, and call the fire department out for a rescue. No one did. Soon he was almost hypothermic. It was getting dark and he had to get off the ice, as it was now beginning to break up. He knew the surrounding slush would push him downriver. About 200 yards below him was a set of rapids with large roiling haystacks. If he made it through the stacks—which was extremely doubtful—in another hundred yards he'd be out into the lake, trapped below the edge of the miles of lake ice.

Realizing he was out of options—and time—he stepped off into the pocket behind the iceberg, composed himself, made peace with the Big Guy and then waded into the slush. It pulled his feet out from underneath him and drove the tip of his rod into the riverbed. When it sprang back up, the hook drove itself through his bottom lip. Luckily he managed to get to the shore about 10 yards short of the haystacks and certain death. By the time he walked back to the car, his jacket was frozen solid and he had a decidedly purple tinge. He drove into a nearby town and thawed himself out.

My brush with death happened when I was fishing in the Niagara Gorge for winter steelhead and salmon. I was with a woman who was doing exceptionally well, taking three fish in three casts—very unusual in that watershed—and I'd helped her land them. I still hadn't had the chance to set up my rod. And, due to the activity of running around and helping her land the fish, I'd become quite warm and removed my thick, heavy jacket plus the two sweaters I was wearing. Inside the gorge, it is usually quite warm, and it is often possible to fish there in February wearing a sweater. On her next drift, she hooked into something big and, not wanting to lose it, handed me the rod to play it out. I stepped back onto what I thought was an ice-covered rock, but busted through a thin sheet of ice and fell into the Niagara River. On the way in, I took a deep breath, figuring once I hit the water I'd be too cold to inhale.

I popped to the surface, traveling at a hell of a rate, all the while struggling to keep afloat. As I was being pushed further out into the swells and massive mud-colored waves, all I could think of was, "Shit, this is loud" and "Shit, the last thing I'm gonna see is a bunch of sea gulls. Oh well!" Then the current pulled me back toward the shore. As soon as my feet hit the gravel and beach boulders, I scrambled for dear life until I was on the shore. As I escaped from the water—shaking like a grizzly bear—several other anglers who had seen what was going on grabbed my jacket and sweaters and were running along the shore to meet me. I stripped off, dried myself with one sweater, then slipped into the other one and my jacket. Walking barefoot through the snow, 300 or 400 yards up the side of the gorge to the car, was nothing more than a slight inconvenience compared with what I'd just gone through. Back at the car, I hugged the dashboard heater until all the fishing gear and wet clothing had been loaded into the trunk. We drove back to Guelph—a two-hour trip—and wearing only a sweater, I vowed with each passing mile that it was the last time I would fish in the gorge. It was—although, since then, I have fished many times several miles above the Falls for both smallmouth bass and steelhead.

Les and I agreed that on these occasions, *all* our guardian angels had been working overtime.

Funnily enough, a couple of years later, and at almost the same spot in the Niagara River where I'd gone for a dip, Wee Dougie, a float fisherman I tie flies for, was drifting for bass on a warm summer day. Out of nowhere, there were people running around, and a large silver barrel floated up to the shore. The hatch was popped open and a very confused-looking chap, bleeding around the head, was extracted from the barrel and dragged away. Dougie just went on fishing. Minutes later, as a chopper hovered overhead, the police arrived, screaming and yelling into walkie-talkies and at Dougie, asking him if he had seen what happened.

Thinking an answer of "yes" might screw up his day of fishing, he went with, "Can't tell ya anything; that thing was laying there before I got here. Thought I'd fish around it just in case any smallmouth were using it as a current break. You'd think someone would clean up that crap, or at least float it over to the U.S. side. It's gotta be bad for Canadian tourism." Then he asked the cops if they knew of any hot fly patterns for catching bass. As he put it, "Well, they were standing right there!" Given the circumstances, most fishermen would do the same. Later he found out the police were going to charge the daredevil, under the

Niagara Parks Act, with "stunting," which carries a fine of $10,000.

"Hey, Les! I'm still getting small stuff. How many do you think we're up to?"

"Probably well over a hundred."

"That's what I figure. Too bad we only caught the one monster up in the slop." This was a direct dig at the fact that we couldn't get a decent number of larger fish, those over 15 inches, from the water we had been covering. It would not be unreasonable to expect there should have *easily* been a dozen or so fish of that quality. To miss getting large fish from the water we had just fished over was beyond comprehension.

"Ian, I'm starting to think—idiots."

"Hey, I'm thinking—clowns."

By now we were across from a golf course, and could hear the loud and sharp whacking of balls. Les was 15 yards in front of me, working a nice slack section, tucked in between some fast broken water and the edge of a grove of willow trees. Suddenly, to get my attention, he was waving both arms starting a game of angling charades. He gave me the arms-wide-open sign—big fish—followed by a Pinocchio-nose sign—gar pike. These were followed by a finger to the lips—a stealthy approach—and finally a wave combined with a point to the back of his waders—get my ass over to where he was. On the way there, I was watching him casting, noticing he was using very slow movements, so I knew the fish were all around him and thus easily spooked.

When I got beside him, I realized he had discovered the mother of all long-nose gar-pike pools. They were thick in the water. Sunning themselves inches below the water and gulping air with their long snouts—hence the name—they were leaving their tell-tale calling-card: a single bubble on the surface. Since 1979, when I'd seen Ginny—a schoolteacher from Campbellford, fishing near the town of Hastings—catch one of the first ones in southern Ontario on a fly, these fish had become one of my addictions. But never in all my years of fishing for them had I seen this many in one place in a river. (Now, I can find these kinds of numbers, or more, in Lake St. Clair, along edges of Lake Erie, in the Trent–Severn waterway and out at the eastern end of Lake Ontario, but never like this in a river.) Les and I pitched everything we had at them, and all we came up with was a total of eight hits. I tried my never-fail flies like Wee Muddlers, Double Elk Hair Caddis, Klepps Killers and Chartreuse Boobies . . . nothing. A Big Joe's Boatman and the Klinkhamer Special came up short. Not a snout stirred at a size-14 Dexter. They turned up their noses, and they have the noses to do it well, at a Kolking's Caddis. A Claret Dabbler . . . nope! Dunkeld Dabbler . . . bupkis! I was starting to feel like John Cleese in the Monty Python cheese shop. Even my top-secret two-fly system, developed over two decades of trial and error, drew a blank. It was nothing short of humiliating. One fish was almost 4 feet in length, so I knew I'd be coming back to this spot many times over the summer.

Eventually we had to leave, and crossed back to the side of the river where the car was parked. Les had promised the family he would be home at noon, so a hurried trek back along the bank was in order. Standing waist deep in vegetation, with no sign of a trail, not looking forward to the walk back, we gazed out at the manicured fairways and the golfers sitting in their carts, sipping on bottles of water. We could have taken some water with us, but the extra weight would only have slowed us down. Our supply was in a cooler in the trunk, waiting for our parched arrival. Plus, I'd prehydrated with water before I left the house. I said, "Hey, we should join this club."

"I didn't know you golfed."

"I don't, but it would be a great place to park so we could get in to fish this spot. Maybe we could get the lads at the club to install a set of bleachers so that when we're fishing those last two pools, there would be a gallery of folk doing the wave. It's a good mile and a half back to the car and it's gotta be 90 degrees, Les."

"It's easily that far. You might have had a wee touch of the sun. Hey, it's almost high noon, there's no wind and it's got to be *well* over 90 degrees. Plus we're both wearing waders. Actually one of those little golf carts would be ideal for hauling our gear down to the pools. We could get the caddies to hand us the rods." He pulled his rod from an imaginary golf bag. "Les, would you like a white or a chartreuse jig on the end of that flipping stick?"

"I could get used to that."

"They could bring us tall glasses, covered in thick condensation, full of exotic fruit juices, with one of those little bamboo umbrellas in the top. We'll hear the ice chinking in the glasses above the gentle humming of the carts." I swung the tip of my rod at an imaginary ball.

"Yes, Mr. James, an 8-weight is what you want to get you down through those long slow pools. Then I'd recommend a 4-weight for those smaller, faster pockets and riffles." I looked at Les. "I think we've both been out in the sun too long, but, hey, all knowledge comes with a price."

"Yeah, and a little heat stroke never killed anybody. Right?" He had a point.

Scooting upstream, along the edge of a river, is always tricky. Scooting upstream against the current, through an area we'd never fished before,

was trickier. Les took one step and dropped into a hole at the edge of the river, with the water stopping an inch shy of the top of his waders. I looked down at him, extended my hand to help pull him out, saying, "Hey, how the hell did we miss that pocket on the way down?" He scrambled back onto the bank. "Thanks. Thought I was a gonner."

"So did I. Shows you how wrong you can be."

He looked at the river. "That looks like a nice pike hole. Look at the weeds, and that is a hell of a drop-off. We missed it because we came down the middle of the river and fished the opposite bank. You were over there, playing in the slop."

"*Oooo eeeee*! Dat's where I dun gone got ma Big Hog! Y'all come back now." I dropped the southern twang. "This hole was still in shadows, that's why we missed it. The sun was up and we were over there, switching from the surface stuff down to the crayfish imitations. Looking at it from here, I bet we can't get to it from the middle of the river. We'll have to fish it from this side in the spring. It might hold a few pickerel as well as some pike."

"Right enough," he said, checking his vest pockets. "There'll be no weeds."

Les blazed the trail, de-spidering all the way back to the car. On the trek, neither of us could come up with a reasonable explanation as to our lack of large fish.

About four hours later, a very violent thunderstorm packing winds of 120 miles an hour tore across the area. Before it hit, I made myself a coffee and unplugged the computer. Just before I disconnected the phone, I called Les, but got his answering machine: *BEEP!* "Hey, Les, look outside. I think I found the reason why we didn't get any big ones. Bye." I hung up, went outside, moved the car to a treeless spot across the street and then sat on the front porch in a T-shirt and boxer shorts to enjoy my coffee and watch the mayhem. It was one of those times when Nature was anything but disappointing and the roiling sea of black and angry clouds delivered in spades what they were threatening to do. The wind ripped off roofs, downed power lines and did the usual stuff, like pummeling all below with golf-ball-sized hail-stones. It gave the farmers an unexpected and undeserved thumping—they needed this like they needed a hole in the head—by ripping off corn leaves and destroying tomatoes and black tobacco crops: well, there go the ketchup and the cigars of tomorrow. This storm, I'm sure, had sent the big fish sulking down onto the riverbed eight hours or more before it hit.

Midgerigars

ly fishing at night is frightening, very productive and always addictive. Brought on by temporary sensory deprivation and isolation, there is an altered and much heightened state of awareness. Some say that "the dead know nothing," but the Mayans say, "the dead live on." When childhood monsters are once again crawling from beneath the bed and walking on the moonless banks, a snapping twig can make even the hardiest of midnight anglers cringe.

I have a fondness for nocturnal angling, having caught my first fish on a fly after sundown from Scotland's River Clyde when I was six years old. The Clyde is the home of sea trout, grayling and Atlantic salmon, and is the birthplace of the *Queen Elizabeth II* (1965), the *Queen Mary* (1934) and the ill-fated *Lusitania* (1906), conceived and created in the once-great Glasgow shipyards. Had

these lads built the *Titanic*, it probably would still be floating. I didn't know much, or care, about trout, grayling or boats; all I wanted to do was bring home a big salmon—I didn't know much about those either—for my mum.

I'd been fishing all day—actually, casting and scaring fish would be a better way to describe it—and Jimmy, my instructor—having spent most of the day untangling leaders and rescuing flies from trees, rocks and the backs of our sweaters—had all but given up on me. His patience, like the daylight, was quickly disappearing.

Jimmy was almost seventy when he was pressed into service by my da to show me how to fly-fish. Before Jimmy retired, he had worked in the steel mills and had a reputation for being quick with his fists and for having a God-given talent for catching fish. Comments like "Auld Jimmy kin git fish oot a puddle, 'n' the fish dinna even ken thir in there" were not uncommon on the streets of Viewpark. Becoming agitated, he sent me downriver to fish under a bridge. It was the part of the main road going from Motherwell to Hamilton, and a link to the M74 motorway, a major artery running south to England or 20 miles north to Glasgow. Above me, I could hear the echoes of the cars as I read the graffiti. Spray-painted in large blue-and-white letters, the colors of the saltire flag, was an expression of undying and deeply romantic Scottish affection: "Kerry loves Joey." It stood out against the regular scribbles of "Celtic," "Rangers" and "Shug's an arse." Shug's fame is still rampant. Even now, three decades later, his name still appears on walls, tunnels and bus shelters in just about every major Scottish city. According to the writing on the many walls, he is still an arse, but there is some comfort in knowing the lad made a name for himself.

The place was littered with cheap wine and whiskey bottles. There were the remains of fires, the charred, cracked wood and rough ashes a stark contrast to the smooth, gray, fist-sized river pebbles. Chunks of thick green and clear glass sparkled among the boulders like large flat diamonds.

"Mind yi dinna get cut oan that glass. That's enough tae scunner onybody. The arseholes that left that lot must be oot oan a day pass," floated downstream from my mentor.

"Okay." My voice bounced around inside the bridge, then was lost to the breeze and the roar of the traffic.

"And dinna get wet. Yir mum'll kill me."

"Okay." I flipped the cast onto the water. All day long, under Jimmy's instruction, I'd been using a size-8 Peter Ross, and a size-14 Black Gnat, which had "caught lots," but nothing in the way of a fish. I bit the Peter Ross point fly off the line, stuffed it into the pocket of my pants and tied on a size-16 Gravel Bed. The two-fly cast slipped below the surface. Maybe this time I'd get a salmon.

I'd caught lots of fish before this trip. My da had taken my brother and me sea fishing for cod and mackerel in the Clyde Estuary. On a boat out of

Largs, we'd jigged with hand lines, using lures we'd made from bunches of colored elastic bands, and we'd caught eels from the Ardrossan docks on raglan worms. Raglans look like 8-inch-long centipedes, with big nasty pinchers. Dug out of the wet rippled sand during low tide, they were dumped into bright red, yellow-plastic-handled kiddie beach buckets and taken home for bait. We'd caught pike and perch on baggie minnows from the Palis Pond, using an empty wine bottle with the tip of the cone base poked in and baited with lumps of bread. In the mid 60s and early 70s, this pond, several acres of the Clyde valley, and Bothwellhaugh—a mining village of 2,000 people that became extinct in 1959 when, after 75 years, the mine closed—were flooded out to make the man-made loch in the Strathclyde Country Park. At the time, this was one of the biggest land-reclamation projects in the U.K., and it eventually became the rowing venue for the 1974 Common-wealth Games. Today, all that remains of Both-wellhaugh is a one-house museum and a cairn that marks the site of the demolished village.

Now, I'd graduated to fly fishing. As a rite of passage, one fish on a fly and it would be an instant transition to manhood. None of that puberty stuff for me. One fish and I could bullshit with the rest of the men at the pub. Of course, at age six, I was much too young to get into a pub or order a beer—you had to be at *least* eight—but, if I could, I would be able to hold my own. These were the guys with the deerstalkers and the hipwaders. The training wheels were not long off my bike, and I was years away from shaving, but somehow, with one fish, they would call me "Mister."

It was pitch black. Around my hood, the wind howled and the snowflakes stung my face. Georgian Bay in late December is remarkably inhospitable. Raw biting winds and storms appearing out of nowhere make each of these trips an adventure. I was wading the wave-lashed shoreline, fishing for steelhead. Dawn was about four hours away, when the night would evaporate into the low ceiling of gray clouds. If I was lucky, at daybreak, there would be a bright ribbon of sunlight and a brief warm glow. The sun would sneak above the horizon, and, as usual at this time of the year, it would decide it wanted nothing to do with the nasty weather and slip quickly into the thick, gray security blanket above it, staying snuggled away for the rest of the day.

Behind me, the contours of the surrounding ski hills would continually develop out of the blackness, escaping from the night, as the daylight grew stronger. The white ski runs would appear, and, like a giant glove, these manmade fingers would spread across the green hillsides. As light sauntered into the cold pre-morning, the outline of the hills would sharpen. Eventually, with the soft edges of a watercolor, the evergreens would form and fill things out. By then, I'd have about two hours of good fishing left before the light would chase my quarry into deeper water and well out of reach of my most ambitious casts.

This is, for me, the last great frontier of fly fishing; it is thrilling and can be extremely dangerous. It is a most compelling venue for high-stakes, demanding and unsympathetic angling. When a hooked steelhead or a salmon runs into the blackness, veteran anglers become incoherent. No doubt the sensory deprivation and the numbing cold help to heighten the adrenaline rush. Trout fishing pales by comparison. The cute little dry flies, the "Match the hatch mosaic" and the returned 14-inch fish are not cut from this cloth. Even the bold and mighty carp (*Ibustup yourpole*) must step aside. Here, the steelhead and Mother Nature are, without question, driving the bus, and everyone else is clutching the seats. When the water is just above freezing, and the air is well below zero, Georgian Bay can kill you, and, if given the chance, it will.

Wading here in July, fishing for smallmouth, I'd only get wet if I fell in. But not now. In this season of dreary days surrounded by dreary days, the winter water is unforgiving. Fail to give it the respect it deserves, or underrate the underlying dangers, and if you're lucky, and wearing a life jacket, eventually someone will find your body. As a wise angler—some folk may call that an oxymoron—once said, "This is one thing you really don't want to screw up."

The sun had been gone for about an hour but I hadn't noticed it had disappeared, nor that two mallard ducks had floated into where I was standing. Listening to the steady lullaby of the cars passing overhead, my mind was everywhere except on the task at hand. Tug! Tug-tug! Tug-tug-tug—TUG! I could feel the rod tip moving long before it registered. When it did, my voice ricocheted around the concrete; hearing the commotion, the ducks exploded from the water and I just about peed myself. "I got a fish. It's A BIG ONE! I GOT A FISH! I GOT A FISH! GET A NET, JIMMY. IT'S A BIG SALMON! GET A NET!"

To say there was urgency in my voice would be a gross understatement. I'd never hooked an Atlantic salmon before, and I'd never shouted as loudly as I did under that bridge, although I did—with most of Scotland—one year later, in 1967, when Glasgow Celtic scored the winner in the 85th minute of the European Cup final against Inter Milan.

My rod tip was still thumping up and down as I hit my six-year-old panic button. I could hear Jimmy, 50 yards upriver, splashing toward me, his rod and fishing bag having been tossed onto the bank. He was yelling things I should be doing, and I was hearing none of them. Still the rod tossed wildly to and fro. "Fir God's sake, laddie, keep the tip up. Keep the tip up! Dinna gie him oany slack. Let him go if he wants tae run, but keep the bloody tip up!" Breathing heavily, Jimmy was now beside me, the last of his words caught in the smoke from a cigarette still dangling at the corner of his mouth. To finish the short sprint without losing the cigarette was quite remarkable. With one hand, he clutched his chest; with the other, the landing net. In anticipation, it was "open," with the chrome handle fully extended, glistening in the diffused light.

"Where iz he?" Jimmy gasped into another puff of smoke.

"Oot there." Trembling, I pointed into the darkness. With a puzzled look, Jimmy glanced at the rod, then at my reel. Placing the net in the water, the excitement in his voice was gone. "Pull the rod tip ower your heid, 'n' the fish'ill swing in." He placed the net in the water, and I did as he said. He scooped up the net, lifting a shape out of the water. Eager to claim my prize, I dropped the rod onto the stones, waded in past the top of my wellies, and peered over the edge of the dripping net. I could feel the cold water soaking me as I brushed against its sides. "Whitz that?"

"That? That? That's a bloody grayling. That's what that is. I nearly had a bloody heart attack runnin' doon here. I'm getting too auld fur this shite. That's a grayling. An' you're gettin' wet."

"Ho," I said stepping away from the netting. "Are yi sure it's no a salmon?"

"Naw. Naw, it's no a salmon, laddie. Salmon are big 'n' silver. They've got a big square tail; yi can grab it like a handle." He pointed to the fish. "Iz that wee thing big and silver?"

"Naw."

He pulled up the dorsal fin. "Does it have a fin on its back like a sailboat?"

"Aye, it does. Diz that mean itz a salmon?"

"Naw. Grayling have a fin like a sailboat. No salmon. Are yi crystal on that?"

"Aye."

"Even a wee baby salmon'll be as lang as yir leg. Yi'll ken when yi catch a salmon; it'll pull the rod away fi yi."

Wetting his hands, he removed the fish from the net, and the fly from its mouth. "Git yir hands wet." I splashed them in the water. "If they are no wet, y'ill pull the slime aff the fish 'n' it'll die." Then he offered me the fish. When I took it from his large, thick steelworker's hands, the grayling seemed much larger in mine. "It's a wee baby. Put it back in, so it kin grow up." I held the fish, all 5 inches of it. Bathed in the fluorescent glow, it looked beautiful. This was my first fish on a fly. "Put it in, laddie, quick so it disna die. Just hold it in the water 'n' it'll swim awa." I did, and it did.

Jimmy looked at my cast. "Wherz the Peter Ross?"

"I ... er ... I took it aff and tied on a wee Gravel Bed. But I left the Black Gnat on the dropper, like you said." He shook his head. "Bloody kids. If yir spendin' time switchin' flies, ye kanna catch a fish, can yi?"

"Naw."

Sensing my disappointment, Jimmy pulled the cigarette stump from his mouth and flipped it into the river. I watched the tiny orange comet arc, then I heard the hiss as it made contact with the water. He lit another fag, and took a long, deep drag. Through his thick, throaty cough, he said, "Fish seem bigger at night. Remember that, laddie; they aw seem bigger at night. A flyrod's mair sensitive than ony other kind o' pole, so even a wee-totty fish feels like a bus. Now, let's get up 'n' git ma gear before some arseholes away wi' it." He picked up the net and my rod, then added, "Ya done a'right, sonny." As he ruffled up my hair, I felt the full weight of his hand. "Oany body kin make a mistake, an' the only way tae learn iz tae get aff yir arse 'n' try it. Fancy a poke 'a' chips on the way hame, so yi kin dry affa bit, an' yir mum'ill no give me a thumpin' fir letting yi get wet?" I looked up at him. He was surrounded by a veil of smoke. I answered, "Aye."

The thought of my mum, about a half of Jimmy's size, giving him a good skelp 'n' a thumpin' put a smile on my face. Steaming hot chips, drenched in malt vinegar, wrapped in soggy newspaper, stretched the smile from ear to ear. Dodging the bottles, the broken glass and a few piles of empty beer cans, we headed up to where he'd hurriedly discarded his stuff. Above the noise of the passing traffic, I could hear him hacking. Little did I know that a size-14 Gravel Bed and a 5-inch grayling would hook me for life, and that Jimmy's 50-yard smoking sprint had unknowingly erased any desire I'd ever have to light up a fag.

Heading up the well-worn trail from the river, I was trudging three or four steps behind Jimmy. As his smoke settled on the bushes and nettles, he turned, laughing, and said, "Hurry up. The midges 'ill be gettin bad soon."

"Midgerigars!" I said to myself, thinking of the wee black-haired lassie from the land of the Belted Galloway, who had introduced me to the phrase months earlier. "Biting bugs the size o' budgies"— that's what she'd said about them, "The size o' budgies." I turned, taking one last look at the river, wondering if my fish was going to be okay.

The shimmering liquid lights dancing on the black surface would be the roots of my addiction.

Leaving behind the deep water of the bay, the steelhead slipped into the shallows, following its primeval procreational urge. Sleek and silver, silently it moved through its cold steel world. Like a magnet, three days of blowing snow, mixed with freezing rain, had drawn both the fish and myself to the river's mouth. The fish had followed its instincts, and I the blue flashing light of a snow-plow, through the Beaver Valley in the dark wee hours of the morning. On the drive up, the white-outs were getting worse and road conditions were, with each passing mile, quickly deteriorating. I had a passenger seat packed with a week's worth of provisions—including blankets and a small propane stove—should it all go wrong and force me to spend the night huddled in the car. Having done it several times before, I didn't see this as a problem and, although it is not in my top ten list of things to do, it can be quite exciting if you're well prepared. Now, however, my gut feeling—a basic instinct never to be second-guessed—was telling me to find a gas bar, or anything else that was open, and to wait there until the storm subsided just enough to let me get to where I wanted to go. If nothing was open, I'd pull off into any parking lot—more often than not, a farm-machinery dealership—to wait this one out. Eventually I turned the car into the parking lot of a greasy-spoon restaurant and gas bar. There were no tire tracks, the cars were thick with snow, and the light from the windows looked very inviting. I reversed into an area closest to the door—easier to jump-start the car should the need arise—and made a dash for sanctuary. The door slammed shut behind me, and twelve heads turned toward me, one of which I recognized.

"Billy Tumbling Brook," I called out, "my long-lost Native brother, what the hell are you doing here? Haven't seen you in—it's gotta be at least a week."

"Same as you, Man Who Wears a Skirt. Trying to stay attached to my arse, waiting out the storm, so I can get up steelheading. I hear the fish are in, not like our last trip. If I'd known you were gonna be here, I'd have brought you a haggis."

Billy and I had known each other for years. We met through a strange quirk of fate when we discovered we were the only idiots left on a river, just as a massive snowstorm rolled in from Lake Huron. Realizing the trek back to our cars—an hour under summertime conditions—was impossible, we had no choice but to hunker down in the bush until it blew over, almost four hours later. We huddled under a makeshift lean-to—a brush pile—passing the time exchanging Scottish and Indian jokes, trying to one-up each other in both political incorrectness and exquisitely poor taste. It was hilarious, and the experience cemented a bond that grows stronger every year. His comment—"We might be different colors, but our hides are just as thick"—said it all.

Over the winters, on steelheading trips together — he wouldn't fish for any other species, referring to himself as a "Steelhead Snob"—I'd watched him fall into more creeks and streams than I'd care to remember. His attitude of "Being hell-bent on getting to where the fish were" had given him many a good soaker. He once owned a fishing vest with "Go back? Hell no! I just got here!" embroidered on the back. One day I began calling him "Tumbling Brook" and the name stuck. Our relationship was like those of many other anglers in that it was strongest when the fish were in and almost nonexistent when the fish were unavailable.

Billy had a passion for collecting angling gadgets, each with the hope of making him a better fisherman. Often referring to them as the trinkets of the white man, he seldom used them, but, like a magpie, found the small bright objects irresistible. This, and his inability to grow sweetgrass from the transplants I continually gave him, were the sources of many a good ribbing.

"How long have you been stuck here?"

"About an hour. Everything's pretty much plugged up. They pulled the snowplows off the road, and it looks like they won't be going back on for about an hour or two."

"How'd you know that?"

"The guy sleeping in the corner is the dispatcher."

As it turned out, other than the cook, who hadn't quite got around to replacing the bald treads on his car with snowtires, and was stuck when the weather turned bad, and the dispatcher, who misjudged how quickly the conditions had deteriorated, the ten folk sitting around the tables, drinking coffee and eating hamburgers at midnight were fishermen. When the snowplows and sanding trucks finally pulled into the parking lot, the drivers were greeted with loud cheering and high-fives all around. After one last round of coffee, we formed a slow moving "conga line" behind them, inching to where we knew the fish would be.

Lazily, as it hovered in the blackness, the fish picked off a few minnows. There was no need to rush. Here, in 3 feet of water, it was a very efficient predator and the minnows had little chance of escape. At 15 pounds, the steelhead has few natural enemies, his sheer size making him safe from hungry cormorants or other fish. He did have the occasional run in with a lamprey, or a skirmish with a coho or chinook salmon on the spawning redds, but that was about it. He was coming here to run the river and reproduce—to find the gravel bed where he had developed from an opaque orange, pea-sized egg, and begin the cycle again. He would swim many miles upstream to the head-waters, or to a small tributary of the main river. There he'd find a female cleaning out a spawning area, digging a redd with her tail. He'd court her as she worked and, lying beside her, he'd quiver, sliding and twisting along her body. He'd nudge her with his snout. When ready, she'd swim into the middle of the redd, and he'd slip in beside her, pressing his body against hers. Together they would vibrate and arch their bodies. Within seconds it would be over—which, if you think about it, is a bit of a bummer after a 5-mile upstream swim—and the eggs and milt would be released. The fertilized eggs would fall into the crevices and chinks in the gravel that she had so carefully cleaned. She'd swim to the top of her nest and dig up some loose gravel, letting it drift back in the current onto the eggs, hiding them from predators and securing them into the nest.

A minnow twisted in the water. The glint from its body registered in the steelhead's unblinking eye. He flicked his tail, opened his mouth, engulfing the minnow in one smooth and effortless movement.

Like the steelhead, I too had been waiting through the fall for rain. October had been one of the driest on record. November was no better. What little rain had fallen was sucked into the ground like a giant, greedy sponge. Little water, if any, had found its way into the parched river systems of Southern Ontario.

The day-tripper tourists had returned to their cities after having taken in the fall colors. The October trees stood naked, filling the valleys like wisps of thin gray smoke. Amid the barren branches, with conspicuous white bellies, red-tailed hawks waited in patient ambush. These last few birds were toughing it out for a bit longer before heading south. The turkey vultures were long gone. On a bass outing, I'd watched them massing: flocks of fifty to sixty birds, slowly drifting southward; black specks, soaring on the up-drafts against the white October thunderheads.

Through it all, there hadn't been much rain. Patches of soya beans dotting the countryside were never in any danger of rotting in the fields. Farmers in bright red or green combines moved over the land with an ease they hadn't seen in years. Now, the only crops left standing were the rows of dry gray-leafed corn rustling and wind-drying in the fields. So far, the winter winds had brought only light dustings of snow and drifted fallen leaves into crunchy heaps. Throughout November, Nature slowly ground to a halt, waiting for December to arrive. And arrive it did.

The fish didn't know this was the tail end of the first good winter storm that had brought us here. Three feet of snow had been dumped on Denver before it turned northward to the Great Lakes, transforming the province into a Winter Wonderland. In very short order, when it hit, southern Ontario had taken on a Christmas-card feel. I wondered if the fish could taste the snow or smell the rain, which had been so long in coming.

They didn't know I'd ignored the winter-storm warnings, or that the police had closed many of the roads. They didn't know, that across many rural areas, the power lines were down. They didn't know that I had double cream in my coffee or that the girl in the donut-shop take-out window had said, "You must be totally mad," as she handed me my order several hours ago, at the beginning of my trip. Anticipating another easy meal, the fish cruised around the shallows, plucking a few loose salmon eggs off the lakebed.

Soon the steelhead would enter the river mouth, and the monofilament mayhem. It would pass the bait fishermen, with their marshmallows, dew worms, or roe bags containing salmon or trout eggs, who fished stationary on the lakebed. The pier chuckers, the lads throwing plugs and lures, would be the next stage of the gauntlet. Further up the river, using 15-foot noodle rods, there would be the float fishermen. Below fluorescent yellow or orange bobbers, there would be drifting roe bags, or perhaps a fly like a Scud, Red Wiggler or Paul Noble's Freestone Nymph.

This late in the year, and in these malicious conditions, only the diehard anglers are left to fish. The river is free of the fair-weather fishermen. Driving snow and a plummeting mercury are the perfect combination for weeding out the number of anglers on the bank. Where once there were more than a hundred anglers—affectionately called "loogans"—now there will be five. When the big runs of fall salmon start to come in, loogans turn the riverbanks into a hillbilly *Brigadoon*. Lining up shoulder to shoulder, sometimes two rows deep, just in case one of the front row stumbles and the gap has to be filled, loogans specialize in snagging, the fine art of ripping lures and hooks into the backs of fish. "Loogan watching" is a pony show, a constant source of entertainment, provided you keep a safe distance from the pack and observe them only from afar. Broken limbs, busted gear, knifings and streamside beatings are an intricate part of the pack mentality. They have the ability to transform a day of quiet angling into a bout of full-contact fly fishing, so they are best avoided. All loogans are meat fishermen, but not all meat fishermen are loogans. Some meat fishermen—the "I gotta take something home for the freezer otherwise I didn't have a good trip"—do use legal angling methods, but the loogans never do.

Those out fishing when it's 15-below are the addicted, the afflicted and the foolhardy. Mostly men—women are too smart to even *consider* fishing under these conditions—without hope, and usually without replacement batteries for their flashlights, which have just burned out. They know it's the batteries, and everyone around them knows it's the batteries. Still, like giant woodpeckers, they instinctively tap them against the rocks, hoping they will flicker for one more minute. This is the perfect opportunity to utter a few words of encouragement, like: "Ever notice those things don't burn out in the daylight? Must be built-in obsolescence." If Morse Code Morley nods in agreement, it's always fun to follow up with: "Check and see if the connections are good." When it's blowing snow, 10-below, almost pitch black, and the fish "ain't biting worth a ...," watching someone struggling with the internal organs of a flashlight is priceless.

There was nothing around all the insulated clothing I could squeeze into but blackness, waves and wind. Topping my outfit was my woollen pariah toque, made of thick, tan-colored rug wool, sporting a brown fish motif and a big pom-pom. It was handmade for me almost twenty years ago, and had since taken on a life of its own. I am totally convinced of a direct link between its growth and the number of socks in my drawer that go missing.

The drawstrings on my hood were tightened down, but there was just enough exposed skin between the hood and the rim of my glasses to make the stinging sleet unpleasant. My hands, wet from stripping-in the casts and from the spray thrown up against my waders, were numb. I've yet to find a glove worth using when it's like this. A pair of woolen mitts were tucked away in a jacket top pocket, with a good-luck charm, just in case I got too cold and had to warm up my fingers when taking a fishing break. Small chunks of ice were starting to form in the creases of the elbows of my jacket, and all wet spots were now crunchy.

I pulled the tip of the rod out of my mouth and worked the now-melting ice free from the top guide, quickly laying out a murderous cast into the blackness. When it's below zero, ice forms on the guides after four or five casts. I've tried everything to prevent them from freezing—car lubricants, antifreeze and cooking oil—but nothing seems to work. The nice thing about casting when the guides and line have a thin ice skin is that, because there is no friction, the line goes for miles. I was easily getting into my backing, heaving the line and the size-4 Penguin into the wind. After half an hour of pulling flies, I snipped off the Penguin and tied on a size-4 Winkie.

After about an hour of very careful wading, and numerous de-icings of guides and flies, nothing was happening. Moving beneath the waves and swirling snow, the steelhead slipped among the rocks, looking for another easy meal. I started stripping in another long cast. Tug … pause to let the fly sink … tug … pause to let the fly sink. Somewhere, the black and green Winkie twinkled.

Another minnow disappeared.

Tug … tug …

The steelhead turned, leisurely drawing in the fly.

I felt like I'd tapped a weed. But when I lifted the rod there was a violent head shake and 10 yards out a silver torpedo cleared the water. Line started zipping through the guides until a large chunk of ice coating the line wedged itself into the stripper guide. "Rat's arse." Everything tightened up, the fish threw the hook, and both of them dropped through the snowflakes into the inky water. "Awwww."

I spent the next few minutes clearing out the guides. By the time I'd finished, the wind was picking up, and the sleet and snow were chewing at my face. Four or five casts later, I was giving another fish a flossing. This time the guides didn't freeze up, but by the time I had the steelhead close enough to release, I was having a hard time seeing the end of my rod, and my inner voices were yelling, "Leave now, leave now, ya stubborn Scotsman." *This* was the time to clear out—not a minute from now—to avoid becoming completely disoriented and unable to find my way back to the car.

As I turned to the shore, everything seemed more civilized, now that the sleet, snow and wind were battering on the *back* of my hood and I was struggling to keep myself from laying out "just" one or two more casts. The fish I'd released *had* to have a bunch of his buddies hanging around here somewhere. A large wave rolled out of the blackness and tipped me forward. I fell onto my knees, then instantly sprang to my feet. I couldn't find my footing, went down again and got a soaker down the front of my waders. "That's it. I'm outta here! That one was a wee bitty too close." Before the next wave rolled in, I had crawled and scrambled into the shallows and safety, with my heart beating wildly in my head. The shock, more than the power of the wave, had taken me off guard. Had I been in the deeper water, where I was less than two minutes ago, I would have been bobbing for ice-cubes in the surf, which, under the circumstances, would not have been a good thing.

From the direction of the parking lot, a pair of headlights caught my eye. They didn't switch off, but were shining like the landing lights of a 747 dropping through the base of the clouds on a final approach. I stepped out of the water onto the beach, now covered in fresh snow. I was still some 200 yards from the car park, but now at least I had something to aim for, and, more importantly, I was well clear of the water. The wind was screaming off the bay, tearing at my hood and gnawing at my wet hands. I pulled out the thick, woolen mittens and slipped them on, the perception of warmth being greater than the actual increase in temperature. Stumbling over the beach boulders, now hidden and totally covered with snow, I headed toward the lights, with an eerie feeling floating around in the back of my cranium that Georgian Bay was upset at having missed me. Who knows? Maybe it was looking for some type of payback for all the fish I'd caught over the years; maybe it was annoyed that it was under siege from the first storm of the winter and wanted to pick on someone. I had the feeling that everything on the

Bruce Peninsula that wasn't tied down was, with a heel-click, going to end up in Kansas.

I trudged to the parking lot. The lights were attached to a black Mercedes. Snuggled amidst the drifting snow, it looked like an inside-out Oreo cookie. When I was close enough to see inside, the interior light came on, and there sat Billy Tumbling Brook. *Obviously* dry and warm, and *obviously* having a good time, he was tapping out a rhythm on the steering wheel and keeping perfect time with the pounding drums. The window started to slide down; through the gap and above the howling wind came the howling of very loud pow-wow music. *"Hey–he–ya–ya–hey–he–hay!"* He turned down the volume. "Hey, Snow White, you look hideous. Having fun?" Before I could answer, he followed with "Thought you'd be here, 'coz you weren't fishing with me and these are the only two places to find fish. I took three on one of those black Torpedoes you gave me the last time we were out. Small fish, nothing over 5 pounds. The roads are plugging up, so we'll be going noplace for the next few hours if we don't go now. I've got some coffees; figure we'd best head back toward town while we still can. This one's gonna be worse than the last one." He tapped his car like he was petting a horse. "Glad the wife talked me into getting this. Lots of leg room, high resale value *and* a great heater." Again, before I could get a word in, "Jeez, that lake sounds angry; did you piss it off?" I chomped down into the wet woolen mittens clasped between my teeth, *"Mmm–uuu–fff–wwa."* Then, after he'd given me a very puzzled look, I gave up trying to speak. My fingers felt like cardboard as I slipped down my waders and fumbled in the pocket of my insulated track pants for my keys.

Muskie Madness

It was a typical Muskoka daybreak—or it would have been had we been in the Muskokas. We were in a secret location near Pigeon Lake in the Kawarthas, about a three-hour drive north of Toronto. The water was smooth as glass. The horizon, and everything else more than 10 yards from the bow of the boat, was obscured in mist. Back in Scotland it would have been classified as a wee bit of low cloud cover. At the far end of Paul's 10-foot aluminum boat, the *Easy Come Easy Go*, a 15-horse outboard was coaxed to life. "She doesn't like getting wet or these damp mornings," whispered Paul, as if hearing his voice would convince the motor to pack it in for the day.

"Great," I thought. We inched forward into the soft gray sheet. "You sure you know where you're going?"

"Yeah, I grew up on this lake."

An image of my returning to Glasgow after a two-year stay in Canada went through my mind. Things change. Just how good was Paul's memory? I shuddered, but not from the cool morning air. I convinced myself that the sun would burn off the fog and by ten o'clock it should be crystal clear. That still left four hours of playing tag in a minefield of hidden weedbeds, submerged stumps and rocky shoals. If nothing else, it would be entertaining. "Hey, Paul, are you packing extra shear pins for the prop, in case we get busted up on some boulders?"

Grinning, he held up a Ziploc bag full of them. "No worries." His enthusiasm did little to inspire confidence.

I resigned myself to the inevitable. Time is more than a great healer. I thought about asking him when he'd last fished the lake. Then I remembered the deserted mouse nests and the piles of black droppings we had removed from the boat. Gothic were the spiders' webs I had dusted from the motor. "There are some things a man should not know," my father always told me.

We were fishing for muskies. *Muskellunge* (mus-ke.lunj) from the Algonquian, *mas*, great, and *kinong*, pike. Looking at one leaves you in little doubt that the Algonquin were dead-on when they named the beast. In a word, the muskie is best described as "nasty." In two words, "nasty" and "vicious." It is a fish of a thousand casts. A hundred hours of fishing are needed before hooking one. Those who try to catch muskies say they "hunt" them. The anglers who pursue them are solitary, lonesome souls. They are thinkers; or you'd think they'd be thinkers, given that there is a lot of time in-between fish. They often say little and can be recognized at dockside by the "disgruntled postal worker" look in their eyes. They are usually wearing army fatigues and sporting a very large net. Their eyes are as cold and unforgiving as those of the quarry they stalk.

The muskie is a man's fish—big, mean and with a mouthful of reasons for keeping your fingers well clear. At 40 pounds and up to 5 feet in length, the muskie is at the top of the freshwater food chain. And muskies have the attitude to go with it. I've hooked them and watched them swim to the boat with an evil grin and an "I dare you" look about them. Behind them, I imagine, little muskies are swimming along shouting "Go on, Dad. Get him" or "You wanna swim up and watch my mum kick some angler's ass?"

You have to learn how to fish for muskie. The tricks of the trade come through time on the water and experience. Sort of like a young boy figuring out how to wet-shave the nick between nose and top lip without drawing blood. Aggressive feeding stories of the muskie are legion. There are yearly reports of muskie taking small dogs off the surface and documented doctors' evidence of toes bitten while being dangled carelessly over the edge of the cottage dock. I have seen a muskie devour a fully grown male mallard duck from the surface of Lake Simcoe. All I could do was think about tossing the fish a can of orange juice and a box of toothpicks. The great muskie is the number one freshwater species on the "urban legend" list.

Imagine, if you will, Bubba. He's on the beach, vacationing at the family cottage. His undershirt just covers his beer belly, and his white legs stick out below his boxer shorts—looking somewhat like a marshmallow perched on a pair of straws. He's half-asleep, unshaven, scratching himself and suffering from a combination of bed head and a wicked hangover. Halfheartedly, he throws a stick into the lake for the wife's adorable, yappy Chihuahua. It's the species you see being carried around the hardware store. "Does Mummsie's little Snuggums want a treatsie-weetsie?" Snuggled between a protective pair of large bosoms, the mutt yips at you as you pass it by, looking for the "I hope they are out of these, 'coz the football game is on this afternoon and I don't want to fix it" department.

Bubba doesn't like the dog and the dog doesn't like Bubba. The only bond they share is a common fear of Bubba's wife, the dainty Dutch damsel Zelda. This 230-pound bingo-hall beauty watches approvingly from the dock. She's wearing a faded housecoat and toeless pink slippers, and, since her hair is done up in curlers, you know there's a big jackpot tonight. She turns back to the cottage in search of a masonry trowel to apply some makeup.

Bubba strings a few syllables together and mumbles something like "Fetch." Snuggums growls and swims off toward the floating stick. A few strokes of dog paddle and he's become a memory. Yet another urban legend. Swirl, splash, silence. Bubba stares in disbelief "What the ... ?" Then the agonizing wait to see if Snuggums will resurface. Time stands still. Without realizing the gravity of his situation, he falls to his knees. Like Pelé popping the winner in a World Cup final, his arms are raised and his fists clenched. "Yes! YES! YES!" he screams, and 80,000 stadium fans go wild.

"YESSS!" Around the globe millions are watching the slow-motion instant replay. "YESSS!" Birds scatter. Looking like it's in a beer commercial, somewhere in a swamp a moose raises its head. "THANK YOU, GOD," Bubba bellows into the air. "Oh, thank you. OH, THANK YOU, JESUS. YEEEESSSSSSSSSS! Yessiree Bob!" Grinning and punching the air, he turns to see Zelda standing behind him. She's wondering what all the commotion is about. Unless her hair curlers are too tight, she won't take long to figure things out and lay the blame. His words "an act of God" will fall on ears of stone.

I was slapped back to reality when Paul hollered, "Watch the water!" above the protesting squeal of the motor. I just knew it would be happier under a tarp on dry land. "It's everywhere. It's everywhere!" I shouted back. "I'll let you know when it's going to do something it shouldn't be doing." He gave me the "look for stumps and big boulders" look. Sheepishly, I peered over either side. Gray soup. It looked exactly the same over either side. Except for the wake, and the waves disappearing into the enveloping gray soup behind us, everything looked the same. "It'd make a cracking jigsaw puzzle," I thought to myself. Hoping the trip would be relatively lumber free, I resumed my duty.

"I'm gonna check the map."

"Map good. Fog bad," I responded in my best Boris Karloff voice. It was obvious that Paul had no idea where we were. He cut the motor. Silence descended like the fog we were in. "It's a good thing there's not a lot of boat traffic on this lake."

"Traffic bad," I said reaching for my flyrod. He unfolded less than half of what was once a map of the lake.

"Now I know what the little brown buggers used as nesting material."

"Nest bad." I punched the line into the gray wall. The king-size Dexter disappeared, towing the fly line behind it. "I'm thinking, what we need is a seeing-eye duck. You didn't happen to pack one, did you?" I started tugging the fly back toward the boat.

"Looks like a cotton ball in a blizzard," he said, still studying the shredded map. Without lifting his eyes from the paper, he followed with "Maybe a wind will come up?"

"Sure it will, and the Pope will ordain a woman for the priesthood." Paul looked like a Druid studying a set of intestines, intensely searching for some type—any type—of sign.

I picked the line off the water and recast. With a swish, 20 yards of a size-12 floating Spey line disappeared into the fog. Tug, tug. "FISH!" I shouted. "FISH! FISH! I'm into a fish, for God's sake!" With line ripping through the guides like it was attached to a Hells Angel on a Harley, it was hard to imagine it being anything else. Somewhere in the fog, I could feel something furiously shaking its head. The fish was running—there was little doubt about that. Backing was stripping from the reel. I thought, "Buckle up. It's gonna be a long and bumpy ride." I could smell the faint, fragrant, yet distinctive odor of burning oil coming from the drag system. It was the smell of fear. "Kaput" was the word that sprang to mind. I began to recite, like it was a child's nursery rhyme, the somewhat catchy "Kaput, kaput, my reel it went kaput. Kaput, kaput, my reel it went kaput." The fish was gaining speed. I held the rod in a death grip.

It jumped.

I dropped the rod tip to cushion the impact.

The re-entry sounded like a wallowing hippo. I looked at Paul. He looked at me. Through the miracle of telepathy and years of fishing together, our thoughts became one. "Ho, shit. Holy shit!" There was an eerie silence when the fish stopped. I felt like hyperventilating. Paul looked like he *was* hyperventilating. The rod slowly started to curl. It continued to bend down to the handle. This was no ordinary flyrod. This was my custom-built 11-foot 11-weight—the "Double Eleven Special," as I affectionately called her. She had landed lots of Lake Ontario salmon, many in the 30-pound class. But this was different. It looked as if the cork was starting to bend. I wanted to call a ceasefire. All I could say to her now was "Ah'm sorry, lass. Please forgive me."

Paul was sporting a blank, zombie-like expression, one I had never seen before. I assumed his mind had overloaded and, like Elvis, had left the building. I made a mental note not to ask for his assistance should I get this thing near the boat. Then again, the landing net was safely stored some 250 miles away in his garage. Now I really felt like hyperventilating. Realizing we were netless, I made an instant executive, take-charge decision. "Hey. You fancy having a grab at this if I get it close to the boat?" In his present condition, I might just slip this one past him. He nodded his head slightly. On the way down, his jaw closed. On the way up, his mouth opened. I'll take that as a yes, thinking to myself, "Rather his fingers than mine." The rod started to vibrate. Then it shook, violently. Something big. Something very big. Something very big and very angry was on the other end of the line and was in the process of figuring out what it should do about it. I wasn't having *any* warm, fuzzy feelings about *any* of this.

Paul spoke. "You still got that on?" There was hope in his voice, leaning toward "Please let the answer be no." Confidently, I hid the fear in my voice. "Aw, aye, it's still there."

"I think it's sounding."

"What? Jeezus, Paul, you've lost it."

"Sounding. You know when they dive and go deep ..."

"I know what it means, but I didn't know muskies sounded."

He rambled on. "Oh, yeah, they're big into sounding. They're born to sound. They inspired the invention of the submarine." I shot him my "shut it" look. He did.

The fish decided and, having made up its mind, took about a hundred yards of backing off the reel in under fifteen seconds. I'm thinking: commuter train?

Now I could definitely smell the pungent burning oil. A seizure and a meltdown must surely be just around the bend. "Born to sound, my arse," I mumbled. In truth, the muskie is known for its acrobatics. Many an angler has watched the fish transform into a freshwater tarpon or marlin. The leaps are spectacular. Memories of the ferocious, demonic head-shakes will haunt the angler forever. Then there are the antics of the hooked fish. Carp will sound, salmon sulk, smallmouth dive and lake trout fathom, but muskies leap. "Watch he don't get you round the stumps."

"Stumps! What stumps? I can't see five yards out from the boat."

"Neither can I, but there's got to be stumps out there." It was becoming evident that his brain was out of the loop. "Years of therapy for this lad," I thought to myself.

Locked in a Mexican standoff, one fish and one Scotsman, with little chance of celestial intervention, I had an acute feeling that Mr. Pan Demonium might soon be a third person into the boat. I felt grossly inadequate and with insufficient resources to land the fish. Feeling the muskie's power and anger, I watched the rod throb and shake. Thankfully, with Paul's willingness to land the fish, any upcoming bloodletting would be his. I was not overly optimistic about a photo opportunity.

"Fire up the paddle back there, Sparky, and head out after this." I heard Paul slip the oar through the water, the bow crawling toward the fish. I stripped in line, the boat closed in. "Gently, Paul, gently. I don't want to startle this wee beauty." In a few minutes, I had most of the fly line back onto the reel and my stomach was churning. It was spooky. Something would happen. Soon.

Just what that something was, was anyone's guess. In an involuntary response, I held my breath. I don't know why, but it seemed like the right thing to do. Paul backpaddled, stopping the boat. He removed the lens cap from his camera, thus increasing the pressure I was under. "You planning on landing that any time in the next six months? Give the line a 'ping.' It will wake him up a bit." There was taunting in his words, but we both knew that something had to be done. I "pinged." It turned out to be a very bad plan. All hell broke loose. The muskie headed straight for the boat. It ran under the hull, dragging the line behind it. The line tangled in the keel. Everything tightened up. The fish jumped, rocking the boat as it tugged on the line. With a splash and a snap, the fish was gone. "Woooo!" gasped Paul. "Woooo!" I said. Collectively we sounded like the old steam locomotive *The Flying Scotsman* racing through the Scottish borders.

I asked my lungs to breathe.

Two hours later, the fog lifted and, with this, Paul's navigational skills went through the roof as he positioned the boat along the edge of a promising-looking weedbed. We hadn't said much since our train impersonation. He was using a size-2 White Zonker, and I, a size-2 Plonker. We had hooked a few good-sized smallmouth, but the muskie fishing was slow. Painfully slow. By eight in the evening, we'd eaten all our sandwiches, polished off the home-made iced tea and tried every pattern we had in the boat. We'd fished weedbeds, dropoffs, rocky outcrops, flooded cedars, boat docks and swimming platforms, river mouths flowing into the lake and the river flowing out of the lake. Each spot a good-looking muskie location. Big flies, small flies, floating lines, sinking lines—nothing had worked.

Staying in the same spot and hoping that one would just happen to swim past was not an option. Muskie don't travel in a lake the way some predators do. They prefer to sit in one location and ambush prey. Knowing this, we covered a lot of water. We had to go to the fish; the fish wouldn't come to us. The muskies were living up to their "thousand casts" reputation. Numerous pike and smallmouth had found the flies appealing, but not so the elusive muskie. We had one follow a fly, only to turn away when it saw the boat. Paul had submerged his rod tip and moved it through the water in a figure-8 motion, standard protocol for that situation. Often muskie will attack a lure or fly when it is moved in this very erratic manner. This time around, the technique failed, miserably. The fish swam off, probably in search of something squishy, soft and tasty. I pulled Paul's Loch Ness Lemming pattern free from the Styrofoam drying board, tying it on to the leader. Paul selected a number-2 Orange Mugwump, and did the same. Feeling like a quarterback on the wrong side of a 40–4 scoreboard, I threw out a long cast, and thus began the fourth quarter.

The Loch Ness Lemming is a horrendous bit of fly-tying. Paul invented it in 1989 for one of our trips to the St. Clair River, near Sarnia. There, muskie and pike can grow to mammoth proportions. Like a show-and-tell schoolboy, he produced the fly from the back seat of the car. It looked like a small muskrat when he held it up. I raised my eyebrows. He spoke only four words: "Big fish. Big fly." I thought he'd switched to live bait and had a hamper of hamsters hidden in the trunk. Thankfully he had not, as an aggravated hamster would be a darned tricky thing to cast on a flyrod. The Loch Ness Lemming has a total length of 10 inches and is jointed in two places. This articulated juggernaut is constructed using copious amounts of muskrat fur taken from an old jacket. It casts like a pig, but produces large fish. Never has a fly been more appropriately named.

Like the last several hundred casts, nothing exciting happened on the one I was retrieving. We drifted around a point. "Don't bother saying it," I said. He did anyway. "If I were a muskie, I'd be hanging out around here." I'd heard that, or a variation of it, upon arrival at every new location.

"Look at this," he went on. "A weed line about 3 feet down. A deep dropoff to the one side, and a nice pile of lily pads out to the left. A perfect nursery for bait fish, perch and smallmouth bass. Yuuummmm! Taste that chunky goodness."

He was right. It was one great area. If I were a muskie, I'd be hanging out here, too! "Pay careful attention, boy," I said to myself. I pulled the fly from the water and belted it back out some 20 yards from the boat. It landed inches from the edge of the weeds, and about 2 feet over the shallow side of the dropoff. "Perfection," I thought. I could hear Paul cursing about the fly being on his side of the boat. "Hey! It's out further out than you can cast. Take lessons." Being the chap who taught him how to fly-fish gave me license to criticize his casting abilities. "Maybe I should have learned from an Englishman." Oooh, that hurt. "Better let it slide, boy. This spot is just too good," I said to myself. His comment was, however, duly noted, and repercussions would, at some later stage, occur.

With purpose, a large, menacing shape rose from the channel and into view.

"Muskie. Paul, there's a big muskie taking a boo at Nessie." I tried not to sound overly enthusiastic or terrified. He saw it and stripped his line into the boat. I twitched the lemming. The shape hovered higher up in the water column. "Wish I'd brought a shotgun." Paul's words fell on deaf ears. "Christ, it looks like an Apache helicopter." I paid no attention to his mumblings and moved the fly again. The muskie leisurely floated up to within inches of the water surface, positioning itself 2 feet behind Nessie. It was huge—even bigger than I'd expected. It looked scary—about the size of a single-bed mattress. "Wish we had a net," whimpered Paul from the stern of the boat. I said nothing, transfixed at what was happening some 15 yards from where we sat. "What to do, what to do?" ran through my mind.

Suddenly, I was within one move of putting Boris Spassky in checkmate. The question was: which was the right move? It was bomb-disposal stuff. Snip the right wire, you're a hero. Snip the wrong wire, you're a statistic with a two-minute spot on the five o'clock news. The timer is flashing seven, six, five ... "I hate it when this happens," I told myself. "I like it when they just grab it and run. There is no anticipation. 'Smack' and you're into it before you know what's going on. End of conversation."

... four, three, two, one.

SNIP.

I tugged the fly.

CHECKMATE!

There was a huge swirl. The muskie opened its mouth, beginning to inhale the fly. In a heartbeat I successfully pulled the fly clear of the fish. I was too stunned at my stupidity to swear. Spassky smiled, took my queen and said, "Check." In the editing room, the boys were cuing up the explosion footage. I pulled the fly into a hurried backcast, and then delivered it onto the snout of the muskie. Nothing. I twitched the fly. Nothing. I moved the fly about a foot. Nothing. Then the muskie moved toward the fly. I started tugging the fly back toward the boat. The fish followed like a giant, bewildered puppy. The space between the fish and the boat was becoming critical. As soon as it got a look at the boat, it would be gone. This was not turning out to be a feel-good fishing trip. Ten feet from the boat, the fish stopped. I held my breath. I plunged the top of the rod into the water and began the sweeping figure-8 motion.

Sweat poured. I watched the fish. The fish watched the fly.

In my softest, sexiest Scottish accent, I whispered, "Cum oan, cum oan," coaxing the fish, verbally nudging it along, like a lover toward an orgasm.

"Cum oan now. Just ... a ... wee ... bitty ... closer."

WHAM! Jeez, I wished it were always that easy.

WHAM! The hit almost tore the rod from my hands.

It wrestled like a lion dragging down a zebra. I pulled and set the hook. The rod cleared the water. The top 2 feet were smashed off and missing. "YA, BAAAAAAAAAASSSTAAAAAAAAAA AAAAAARRRDD!!" echoed across the lake, rattling cottage windows. I could almost hear the little muskies laughing and cheering on their aquatic hero. Beneath the surface, I imagined the backslapping and high fives all around. The

victory lap was beginning. The full-time scoreboard told the whole story, Fish 1, Ian 0. The muskie had given the fly the evil eye but decided to tackle the flyrod instead. I was way, way, way past being stunned and had now lost the ability to speak.

Luckily my lungs were working of their own accord.

I looked at Paul. Avoiding eye contact, he looked away. The wanton destruction had wiped out any will to fish that I had left. I wanted to dive overboard and deliver a healthy dose of Scottish retribution. I heard Paul fire up the outboard. I cradled the rod in my arms all the way back to the dock. Upon arrival, Paul gently took it from me and placed it in the trunk of the car. I noticed he didn't slip her inside her protective aluminum rod tube. The monitor flatlined. I knew I had made my last cast with my dear old friend.

Later, much later, when we started laughing about it, he suggested a Viking funeral for the rod, which was past repairing. Three weeks later, on a quiet private pond, I watched as flames engulfed the drifting funeral barge. Actually, it was more of a funeral cardboard box, which we wrapped in plastic, stuffed with straw and doused in a highly flammable liquid, but it's the idea that counts. On our second attempt, this time from the *upwind* end of the pond, just as the last wisps of pyre smoke drifted across the water, a Sony radio cassette fired off a taped twenty-one-gun salute. Suddenly, I realized why some anglers "hunt" muskies.

Line Speed

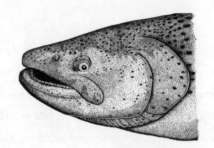

One of the hardest experiences to relate for a fly fisherman is the feeling of terror and helplessness—and the adrenaline rush you get—when you hook a big salmon or steelhead. From the lips of those who have, comments like "I thought I hooked a bus" or "It felt like a Mack truck" are indeed accurate, but they are still lacking. I equate the experience to hooking a greyhound, and I've got the test results to prove it.

Land speed records are often set on the Salt Flats in Utah. There, man and machine challenge the limits, pushing the edges of the envelope until they almost pop. I tested the limits of my fly-fishing gear, and whether or not a hooked salmon does feel like a galloping greyhound, on a windswept sod farm near Bolton, Ontario.

Silently, the rust-splattered white Chevy van rolled slowly through the farm gate, down the long gravel lane, toward the farthest fields. With one hand, Fast Eddie clutched the wheel; with the other, a coffee. I looked out the window. The autumn leaves whirled across the grass and I tried to convince myself: "This is a great idea." Gus, Eddie's four-year-old greyhound, slept in his doggie transportation box. In kiddie lettering and pink paint, "Snowball" was scrawled on the top of the crate. It was going to be a great day.

"Best do this with a tail wind," said Eddie. "Once he feels the wind on his back, he'll fairly pick up the pace." I nodded in agreement. Eddie knew greyhounds. He came from a long line of greyhound owners. He claimed that Gus was a direct descendant of King Death, a celebrated greyhound of the past, and the 1864 winner of the prestigious Waterloo Cup. At the time, this was the U.K.'s Blue Ribbon of the Leash event. It drew the same size crowds as the Stanley Cup hockey final does today.

Of course, there is no direct evidence—something about missing papers and an illegitimate litter—of the century-old canine connection, but if Eddie says it's kosher, then it probably is. For as long as anyone could remember, Eddie's family had raised greyhounds on a farm near Castlebar, on the Irish West Coast. Eddie loved to talk about bloodlines, Welsh coal miners, Irish lords and English earls. Great dogs of the past would pepper his conversation. Faster and Faster, and Master Magrath—the Irish wonder dog—were among his favorites. Master Magrath was so famous, winning the Waterloo Cup an unprecedented three times, that Queen Victoria brought the dog and his trainer to Windsor Castle by royal train, from Lurgan in Ulster, for a private audience. The question begs to be asked: "Did he shake a paw?" Eddie likes to note that Queen Vicki didn't do this when the English dog Fullerton won it four years running from 1889 to 1892. No nationalism there. Then there was Gus.

With the exception of a black splash on his left ear, he was pure white. Eddie had great plans for Gus until his daughters discovered that the dog was cute. Eddie's life fell apart the day he returned home from work to find Gus the greyhound at a tea party, scarfing down fairy cakes and sporting a straw hat. From the look in his kids' eyes, and those of the dog, Eddie knew that all was lost.

Two days after the party, his wife and kids renamed the dog Snowball and he was relocated from the outside kennel to a blanket under the kitchen table. After a month of sleeping on the sofa, Eddie got relocated to the bedroom when he finally succumbed to his wife's pressure and agreed to the dog's name change, but only around the house. Meanwhile, Gus had become accustomed to his new name and the finer things in life. He gave up his training to pursue a full-time position as the family pet. Now his days were filled keeping the backyard free of squirrels, digging up flower beds, taking Eddie's daughters for "draggies" and being the star attraction at "Show and Tell." Whoever coined the phrase "It's a dog's life" must have met Gus the lounge hound. Looking at him now, with his white snout snuggled between his white front paws, it was hard to imagine that, in less than an hour, he'd stride into the annals of canine and fly-fishing history by being the first dog to simulate a salmon.

The van stopped, Gus woke up, and the engine coughed, spluttered, then died. "You get your gear set up and I'll warm up Herr Speedo in the back."

"Fair enough, Eddie," I said, opening the door and stepping down and out. I went around to the back of the van, meeting Eddie at the door latch. He opened it. I reached for my flyrod tube; he unlatched Gus's box. Gus popped out like a jack-in-the-box. His nose was everywhere at the same time, his tongue licked Eddie's face, then his hands, then my hands, and was stretching out for my face when he decided to vacate the van instead. "Bloody dog," said Eddie, wiping dog slime from his face. "That thing's ancestors'll be spinning in their little doggie graves. He's a goof." I had to agree. The royal bloodline had been well watered down by the time it reached Gus.

"All the same, Eddie, he's great with the kids."

"Sure enough, but the kennel club would pull his membership card if they saw him. FETCH, GUS!" With those words he pulled a ball from his jacket pocket, gave a shrill whistle and pitched it across the field. Gus bounded after it. In a few strides he'd returned to the van, circled it, then pissed on one of the back tires. "I'll get you over at the far side of the field." I nodded. "Atta boy. Drop it." Gus did. His tail—a blur of unbridled excitement—looked like it was about to fly off. "Git after it, boy. Git it. Bring it back. Bring it back. Git it." Gus set off after the ball, and Eddie set off for the far side of the field. I remembered the men who walked greyhounds in my youth.

It was blustery, cold and wet. A typical West-of-Scotland, November morning. The sky was the color of dirty concrete. The clouds were pregnant and black. Racing across the sky, they pelted the Clyde Valley with rain, bits of sleet and anything else they had up there. The trees were bare. The leaves stuck to the pavement like post-wedding confetti. Car tires hissed on the road as they passed. Dressed in my high-school uniform, I huddled into a dirty gray bus stop on Old Edinburgh Road, scanning the graffiti to see if any of it was fresh from the previous night. My oasis would be the 240, a double-decker, bright red bus, heading from Glasgow to Lanark. It usually passed through Viewpark at five-thirty. The doors would open, I'd step into the bright, warm interior, flashing the driver my school pass. He'd usually grumble, saying, "Hey! Ye canna use that pass till eight. Mind you, it's your arse that's oot the door if the inspector gits oan. An' dinna say I dinna warn yi." I'd climb the steps, saying, "Thanks, Jimmy," and look for a window seat.

The use of "Jimmy" is peculiar to the Glasgow area. It's used by males approaching other males when help is needed. It's both a form of respect and "I come in peace." For example, when approaching a total stranger on Buchanan Street, in the heart of downtown Glasgow, one might say, "Hey, Jimmy, it's raining. You got any idea where Josylin Square is?" Hearing this, the chap recognizes that you are "local" and will give you the straight goods. It's also a friendly ice-breaker: "Hey, Jimmy, any idea of the time?" "Hey, Jimmy, any idea where the Glasgow School of Art is?" Know that if you ask a question like this, the response will be something like "It's exactly where Charles Rennie Mackintosh built it in 1899."

"Jimmy" can be interchanged with the word "pal." But be forewarned: "pal," when properly used, is a precursor to some type of altercation. "Hey, pal, I just thought I'd let yi know, if yir dug gits intae ma backyard again, I'm gauna shoot it. Okay?" On the river, enjoying the solitude of a wee bit of grayling or sea-trout fishing, one might say to the leather-clad ashen-faced male sporting tricolored hair and a nose ring, "Hey, pal, yir no plannin' oan settin' up that ghetto-blaster here, are yi?"

The bus was usually full of men heading for the steel plants of Motherwell. Upstairs was always packed. They could smoke up there. The lung-wrenching coughing of the chain-smoking chorus could be easily heard from my downstairs seat. It's little wonder that the West of Scotland once held the world record for the highest rate of lung cancer per head of population. I liked to peer out the window. Sometimes, I'd watch the dawn breaking—a thin orange ribbon behind the black cooling towers, coke piles and cranes of the steel mills. If the air was heavy and still with a winter frost, the last few stars would still be visible. Venus would sparkle in the pre-dawn rosy glow. As the bus rolled out of Bellshill, down the Motherwell Road, crossing the bridge at the River Calder, I'd sometimes see a rabbit or two in the fields going up the hill into Forgewood. They'd scurry into the thorny gorse bushes. You'll only try to walk through gorse once. It is best described as "Scottish cactus," and well left alone.

Every morning, two men would pass the bus stop, taking eight greyhounds for a walk. Each man had two leashes, with two dogs collared on each leash. One chap would hand his leashes to his partner and he'd trap them under his boot on the sidewalk. He'd stand there, surrounded by dogs, as his friend disappeared into the newspaper shop for two packs of fags. The dogs seemed uninterested in the whole affair, hardly stirring when he returned. The smokes would get opened and each chap would light up. Slightly "steaming" in the cool air, the dogs would look around. Standing 30 inches at the shoulder and weighing in at around 60 pounds, greyhounds know they are cool. They are among the world's fastest dogs, reaching speeds in excess of 40 miles an hour. These are the "top guns" of the canine world.

There was an unwritten local law that you never bothered a man walking greyhounds. It's not that they're ferocious beasts, but, if they were out on a training walk, like the gorse, they were best left alone. One chap pulled down his bunnet, turned up his coat collar, then picked up the leashes from the sidewalk. For the first time in over a year he spoke: "Whit are yi dain' up at this time o' the mornin', sonny?"

"Gauin' swimin'," I said, hoping the bus would not show up.

"Swimmin'? Kin yi no go tae the baths aftir school?"

"Naw, I'm practicin'. I swim fir the school and

fir the Motherwell Club. Nice dugs. How far di yi walk them?"

"Aboot 6 miles a day," his partner replied. Then he added, "Are you Big Joe's boy?"

"Aye."

"I went tae school wi yir da."

"Oh aye." Then I thought to myself: "In this small neighborhood, who didnae?"

He turned to his buddy. "This is Auld Joe Pupkis's grandson. Your faither and Auld Joe worked in the mines the gither. Izat yir bus comin'?"

"Aye, if it's the 240."

It was. As it slowed down, I heard him shout "Git Auld Joe tae bring yi doon tae the kennels ony time. Tell him Wee Tam Mackintyre said it wiz okay." The bus stopped, the doors opened, and I shouted, "Thanks." The driver glared, "No' you again!" I held up my pass, "Itz aw right, Jimmy. The inspector saw it last week 'n' he said it wiz okay. Gez a wee break!" Smiling, he shook his head, "Aye, 'n' I'm Robert the %@!#**! Bruce 'n' this bus is gauin tae Bannockburn." I smiled at him,

stepping into the light and the all-too-familiar pre-dawn chorus. In the weeks that followed, Wee Tam and my granda introduced me to greyhounds.

Rising up before the bounding Gus, it was the *caw-caw-caw* from the scattering crows that snapped me back to the sod farm. The Egyptians started raising greyhounds more than 5,000 years ago, and, over the years, they have been used to hunt everything from stags to wolves, foxes and hares. Looking at Gus "louping" after the airborne crows, I began wondering: "Where had it all gone wrong?"

I assembled my salmon rod, stuck the reel and a spool of 10-pound monofilament into my pocket, and headed upwind, toward Eddie and Gus. Watching the dog sprinting and galloping just for the fun of it, I'm sure he was laughing. He'd chase leaves, stop on a dime, and then twist around, sending up a small shower of grass. With his paws groping the ground for traction, he had the look about him of a dog hanging its head from the window of a speeding car. I've never seen a greyhound do this. I think it's because they have the speed to do it, without the need for a set of wheels. Dolphins are to water as greyhounds are to turf.

I gave myself a pat on the back for selecting the breed as part of my soon-to-be-tested hypothesis. A few times, he used me as a turning beacon. Sprinting toward me at full speed, he rounded me. He was just on the edge of "losing it," going into a high-speed wobble and becoming a tumbleweed of flailing paws and tail. His head was leaning into where I stood. His body was leaning out, pulled by the centrifugal force of the turn he was in. He looked as if his legs and paws were horizontal. He looked like he was having fun. He shot out of the curve like a cyclist "dropping down the track" at a velodrome, and accelerated back down toward the far end of the field. I remembered what I'd heard about "speeds of 40 miles an hour." A quick bit of arithmetic put that at about 65 kilometers an hour. I hit my mental panic button, saying to myself, "I've got about 300 meters of backing on the reel. So, 65 kilometers per hour, divided by 0.3 of a kilometer, gives me about 217 seconds,

divided by 60 seconds to the minute, which is about 3.5 minutes. Shit. That can't be right. Start again, James, and talk yourself through it. Speed equals the distance divided by the time. That much we know for sure. So, the amount of time it's going to take Gus to cover 300 meters is what I need to find out. Time equals the distance divided by the average speed. Fair enough. Step aside, Einstein. Length of backing, 0.3 of a kilo-meter, divided by 65 kilometers per hour, that's about—I need a calculator." Wandering back to the van, I found one in the glove compartment. I punched in the numbers. Twenty-seven seconds. My brain went into shock. As I watched the white blur flying across the grass, my granda smiled through years of memories.

One morning, Wee Tam had given me a hot tip for my granda. "Next time King Blotto's runnin', tell Auld Joe tae bet it. Tell him it'll hae big odds. It's a big white Irish dug. Tell him no tae worry 'n' bet it, 'n' dinna be tellin' onybody else. Are yi clear on that?" "Crystal," I replied. Later that day, on the way home from school, I passed on the message. Months later King Blotto showed up on a mid-afternoon race card in London. Aggravation, an English dog, was the odds-on favorite at two-to-one. King Blotto was listed at sixty-to-one. I skipped school for the afternoon, caught an early bus back to Viewpark, and went to my granda's house to watch the race.

Opening the door, I was greeted with: "Wit are yi dain' back fi school si early? Are you doggin' it? Before yi answer, yi might want tae have a wee think aboot whit yir gauna say. Whit classes are yi missin'?"

"German and French," I said.

"Christ, whit dae the Germans know? Lost baith wars. When the war started Di Gall ran away tae England. Left his comrades tae dook it oot wi the hapless Gerries. He's having tea wi the Royals, while the Gerries are marching up Chanda-leez-a and gettin' their photies taken at the Eiffel Tower. So yir no missin' much either way. Come in and get me a cuppa tea before yi sit doon."

"Nae problem, Granda."

"While yir up, git a bucket of coal oot the bunker and gie the fire a stoke. Dinnae fill the bucket wi dross. That small shite'll no burn."

By the time I'd stoked the fire and made the tea, it was race time. "That Blotto's got some set of back legs on it. Look at the size o' its chest. Aggravation's the home-town favorite. Whit dae the English know aboot racin' dugs? Look at that Irish hound. He's as keen as a groom on his honey-moon. Look at the desire in that dug's eyes. It's a cracker o' a beast."

Aggravation led from the get-go. King Blotto was nowhere until they rounded the last curve, hitting the home straight. Granda was shouting at the top of his lungs: "Come on. Run. Run ya big Irish dug. Run!" It was neck-and-neck by the time they crossed the line. "It's Blotto on the outside, Aggravation on the inside. Blotto. Aggravation. Blotto. Aggravation. Blotto … we'll need a photo to call that one," gasped an out-of-breath announcer.

"Photy, my arse. Blotto's a certainty. Nip up tae the bookie an' git ma winnin's. An' dinna come doon by till it's time fir yi tae be gittin' hame fae school. If your granny finds oot I've been harborin' a criminal, we're baith up shite creek. Yi got that?"

"Yip."

"Make sure yi wash oot yir cup, dry it and stick it back where yi got it. And pit the bucket back in the coal bunker. She's gittin' smarter in her auld age."

"Right, Granda."

The commentator piped up from the TV, "Well, that was an amazing run from the Irish dog." Granda cut him off with "If it wis that amazin', I'd be getting a vet tae check up its arse fir an engine."

"One of the most exciting races we've seen in years," droned the announcer. "Out of the gate at sixty-to-one, who'd have thought that Blotto had talent like that? Quite the sleeper."

Again, Granda was quick to answer his comments. "The only thing oot there that's a sleeper is the judge lookin' at the photy. He must be drinkin' warm milk. I've no got mi glasses on, 'n' I kin tell yi that Blotto won fir sure."

"I've just been informed that Aggravation wins it by a whisker," continued the commentator.

"Aggravation!" shouted Granda, "I'll gie yi 'aggravation.' Whisker, ma arse. Fixed as all hell. They'll no let an Irish dug win in England. Blotto, ma arse. I can run faster than that dug, 'n' I use a cane. Saint Pat shoulda chased the greyhounds oot o' Ireland when he did in the snakes."

"Whit,"—he shifted in his chair—"Whit dae the Irish know aboot dugs? Nuthin'! King Blotto looked like a coo before the start o' the race. A big, bloated, bovine. It ran like a walrus. There wir nae visible signs o' life in that dug's eyes when it got intae the startin' gate. The Irish, they canna even make good whiskey. Aw thir good fir is burnin' peat. It's a nation of sod burners. Sod burners, I tell yi. Irish eyes are smilin' aw'right, 'coz their aw high fi sniffin' sod. Someone should pull the plug oot o' the Emerald Isle, and let it sink intae the Atlantic. They'd be dae'n dug racin' a big favor. Christ! I just gave that big, fat-arsed bookie a quid o' ma hard-earned pension. Wait till I git ma hands on Wee Tam!

I'll knock his heid oot fae underneath his bunnet."

"See yi later, Granda. Yi might want tae throw yir bookie's line in the fire."

"Right enough, sonny, burn the evidence. See yi later oan. Thanks fir the tea. Don't you forget tae dry that mug, or ma arse'll be oot the windie, and you'll no be able to go fly-fishin' till yer bandages cume aff."

"Okay, Granda. See yi."

"See yi." Then he added: "Ony chance o' yi thrown' a haunfi o' grain at ma pigeons oan the way oot?"

"Nae chance, Granda." Then I thought about my supply of feathers for tying soft hackled wets and added, "I'll cume back after dinner. Cheerio!" Chuckling, I dried the mug, put it away and closed the kitchen door behind me. Irish honor and Wee Tam's reputation were restored several weeks later, when Dublin's Pride romped home as a fifty-to-one shot in London. Convinced that there might be a tickertape parade, Granda tried in vain to coax Granny into taking a trip to the Irish capital. And for me, it was the first time I tasted Irish whiskey.

I was laughing by the time I reached Eddie.

"What are you smiling at?"

"I'll tell you on the way home."

"Why'd you go back to the van? I thought you were gonna chicken out."

"Naw. I needed a calculator to work out how fast Gus'll peel the line off my fly reel."

"You'll not need a calculator for that. Fire away," said a very cocky Eddie.

"How long is your line?"

"About 300 meters."

"If Gus gets up to full speed, you'll have about thirty seconds. Right?"

"I'm impressed."

"No need. Dog racin's a game o' inches 'n' seconds. You don't tell me about dugs and I'll no tell you about fishin'."

As the white comet streaked across the top of the field, I turned to Eddie. "The last dog I saw move like that was King Blotto, when I was still in high school. Speaking of man's best friend, is he warmed up?"

"Like a loaf in the oven, like a loaf." Eddie whistled. Without breaking stride, Gus veered to his left and closed in on us. "He uses his tail as a rudder; helps him balance and fine-tune his turns." As he bore down on us, I clenched my teeth, waiting for the impact. At 12 feet out, Gus was showing little sign of slowing down. One stride later, he hit the brakes and stopped inches in front of Eddie. He wrestled with the dog's head. "Atta boy! Good dog." Slobber, slobber, pant, pant. Gus's paws were on Eddie's chest, "Down, doggie! Down, ya big mutt. Down. Git down, ya big goof!" Playfully wrestling the dog, Eddie turned and said, "He's wired."

"No guff. What was your first clue?"

Eddie pulled and pushed at the dog. The harder he thrust Gus away, the more the dog enjoyed it. Teasing him with the ball, Eddie went on: "You want it? Huh? Huh? Grab it then. Come on. Grab it." It was starting to take on the look of a shark feeding frenzy. "Get it, Gus. Ian wants a

lively dog. Let's get you up to speed. Grab it. Come on, doggie. Grab it!" Eddie pushed the dog down and knelt beside him. Gus rolled and was on top of Eddie faster than a rugby prop, or a forward, dropping on a loose ball. Laughing and trying to fend off the onslaught of licks, Eddie gave in. "Okay. Okay. Okay. Good boy! Good Gussy, good boy." Hearing the change in Eddie's voice, Gus slowed down. Dusting himself off, Eddie stood up. "Are you ready?"

"Just about." I snugged the reel into the reel seat and strung the line through the guides.

To one end of my 12-foot leader I tied the fly line, to the other, Gus.

The plan was simple. At about 300 meters, Eddie would stop and wave once. If things were okay, I'd wave my right arm and the rod. He'd begin counting backwards from ten; at four, he'd raise his arms; at zero, his arms would fall and he'd whistle for Gus; and, after that, who knows?

The idea was simple. I wanted to see if a 60-pound greyhound, accelerating down a field, would match the run of a hooked chinook salmon or steelhead. I looked around. Except for the displaced crows, now sitting in the top branches of a maple, the place was deserted. Where was the world's press when you needed it? One way or the other, history was in the making. There would be no black-and-white, scratched, grainy footage to record the auspicious occasion. Intercranially, Mozart's "Turkish Rondo" danced lively. The perfect soundtrack. Gus leaned against my left leg. Instinctively, I rubbed his ears. His eyes were firmly fixed on Eddie. Above the fast-paced notes, Eddie's last words rolled across my brain. His instructions were crystal. "You"—he pointed to the dog—"stay. You"—he pointed to me—"let go of his collar and say, 'Get him!'"

Eddie stopped and waved. I waved. Gus lurched forward, stopping at the length of my left arm. The music stopped. I started the countdown. Eddie raised his arms. Nervously, I looked at the drag setting on my reel. Arms down. I let the thin strip of leather slip from my hands. "Get him!" I said, thinking that, if he didn't want to go, that would be fine too ... Gus tore up the turf. In a couple of

blinks, the fly line dissolved from the reel. Backing was screaming off the spool. I was telling myself to keep the rod up and not to give him any slack, as I would do with a hooked salmon. I tried to keep the tip up, but Gus was making sure that the rod was not going to straighten up above horizontal. I touched the side of the reel. It was hot. Very hot. It was making noises I'd never heard it make before. Gus had no intention of slowing down. I tried to lift the rod tip. It was, as they say, like pissing into the wind. The reel was howling, protesting against the abuse it was experiencing. All I could do was think, "Jeezus!" Gus was fast approaching Eddie, and things were looking not too bad until Eddie pulled the ball from his pocket and threw it.

Gus flew past Eddie.

Just about then, I ran out of line.

The rod snapped to attention as the last turn of backing slipped from the masking tape holding it to the reel. I watched it shoot through the rod tip and begin dancing across the grass. Gus, with the long white ribbon dragging behind him, was gaining on the ball. He caught it, turned and headed back toward Eddie. Straight into a 300-meter nightmare.

I thought about watching, then closed my eyes.

It took me longer than twenty-eight seconds to reach Gus, Eddie and the mangled bird's nest that was once a fly line and backing. I had to laugh when I got there. "What a mess" was my only thought.

"How'd we do?" inquired Eddie.

"What in God's name possessed you to pull a stunt like that?"

"I wanted to see how you'd react to a crisis situation, to throw a little of the 'unexpected' into the equation. When you hook a steelhead, have you ever known exactly what it was going to do?" He had me there. "If I'd told you, it wouldn't have been the same." He had me again. "If I were going salmon fishing, I'd have my equipment warranty cards in my back pocket. Boy, was he flying!"

Scooping the line into my arms, clutching it in a bear hug, I headed back to the van, thinking Auld Joe would have said it best: "It's great stuff fir hawdn' up glad's and dahlie's." By the time I reached the back doors of the Chevy, having proved conclusively that hooking a large Great Lakes salmon or steelhead is like trying to slow down a greyhound, Gus was once again circling the wagon and the crows were long gone.

It is safe to say it's something to think about when you're pondering purchasing a rod and reel for this type of fishing. Take some advice and "Go Big." Fishing the break walls at Owen Sound, Toronto and Thornbury, I've watched fish empty 150 yards of line from my reel in about the same amount of time as Gus did. Fly fishing the shore lines of the Great Lakes is, in my opinion, one of the greatest challenges in freshwater fly fishing. But that's only my opinion. If you're going to try it, make sure you've got lots of backing and you know exactly where your equipment warranty cards are. For the record, the Irish know lots about 'dugs' and their whiskey is not that bad. If you've never been to Ireland, it's a grand place for a visit. I saved my fly line, but the backing was reduced to garden twine. At the time of writing, Gus still sleeps in the kitchen, enjoys the occasional fairy cake and when given the chance chases, but has yet to catch, crows.

Hillbilly Trout

In Ontario, in July, fishing for speckled trout can be painfully slow. Water levels drop, and the rivers show their bare, bleached bones. Though the bright, sunny days may be good for tanning, or for transforming fields of barley into swaying golden seas, they do little to enhance the fishing. But, all in all, it's a pretty season to fish for very pretty fish. Whatever you want to call them—specks, square-tails or brookies—these fish are gorgeous. Their backs are dark green and brown—so dark that they appear to be black. Their sides turn to silver and they have snow-white tummies. They look as if they are covered in camouflage netting, or have the dark-olive and earth-brown patterns of a Spitfire's fuselage. Iridescent red and blue spots are speckled along the sides. Holding one of these fish is unforgettable: It's like watching sunlight dance through a bag of marbles.

In July, the stream banks are lined with flowering yellow flag and blue flag. Cattail heads are firm and brown. In the woods, the spring ostrich-fern fiddleheads have now unfurled to their full 4-foot height. Black-eyed Susans have red admirals fluttering around them. The orange butterfly wings and the yellow daisy petals paint a spectacular canvas. Bees and wasps are everywhere. Blue damselflies, and darters with bodies of gold, green and red, sun themselves on the lush streamside vegetation. Cow parsley towers 8 feet high. There are thick carpets of wild mint. Milkweed, long past the edible-shoot stage, has crowns of purple flowers. On one plant in front of me, the leaves are being eaten by the caterpillars of the monarch butterfly. These cute, 3-inch-long critters are putting on weight before they do the age-old "wing sprouting" thing. Sitting on a moss-covered rock, listening to the gurgling stream, I watch them. As they methodically turn the leaves into a patch of fragile green lace, I'm entertaining heretical thoughts: "Returning to the barbarism of bait fishing might not be a bad idea after all." There are days when Stephan and I can easily catch twenty or thirty specks out of this stretch of the creek, on just about any fly. By the looks of things, after eight hours of fishing without a "tap," today is not going to be one of them.

Too small, forgotten or deliberately left out by the tourism board, you'll never see the towns in this area on a road map. Towns here are far above the Canadian national average for households containing checkered flannel shirts, coon hounds and front-porch beer fridges. Everyone's related and the family trees contain few branches. On a continuous chromosomal loop, the gene pool is dammed up by a bottle neck. Sisters look like brothers, brothers look like fathers, and husbands look like wives. If Darwin had made it up here before going to the Galapagos, science might never have been the same.

The towns live under the constant threat of the paved roads going in, ruining the area's language, culture, charm and beloved isolation. That thin layer of black asphalt could destroy a county, built for generations on a moonshine economy, and in the process ruin a brilliant, relatively unknown speck fishery.

Once they get to know you, the folk are friendly and have a wicked sense of humor. Just outside of town, a big bright yellow road sign states: "No winter maintenance beyond this point." Nailed on the post below it, a chunk of plywood adds: "Good luck."

I'd been introduced to the townsfolk by Linda, one of the local girls. Attending agricultural college in 1981, I'd had a brief fling with this big-eyed, raven-haired, enthusiastic, drop-dead-gorgeous girl. We had a whirlwind romance lasting four weeks, until she flunked out after midterms. One morning over breakfast, somewhere between "Pass the toast" and "Another waffle, please," she added: "You're the first man I've slept with that wasn't family." I felt almost privileged and somehow special, handing her the toast.

On my first trip back to "the farm" with Linda, I found myself in the barn, helping her father castrate piglets. Impressed with my ability to wield a scalpel and perform the task single-handedly, he told me, "If ya want to fish 'round here boy"—Squeeeeeeeeel!—"Hold it, piggie. You just mention my name. Gimme the iodine, will ya?" Out here there was respect for a family name, or the size of a man's biceps. Now, many years later, it was at the back of Linda's father's farm where Stephan, one of my ace fishing buddies and a convert to the joys of carping, and I were fishing. He has a fabulous sense of humor and on just about every trip we've been doubled over, crying with laughter at one of our disasters. He coined the phrase "Uh-oh! It's heading to the bad place," which we've used to describe the reel-smashing runs of a 38-pound salmon, a 40-pound carp, an 18-pound channel cat and several other large things with fins hooked on a fly, but thankfully never seen.

As for Linda, after her dishonorable discharge, she went on to study tinsmithing and welding in Toronto. In 1985 she returned to the homestead, where she now makes a fortune manufacturing moonshine kettles for the locals. She skis all winter in France. I bring bacon sandwiches when I fish here.

This part of Ontario is full of babbling brooks, and free from heavy agricultural or industrial use. It is jam-packed with dense cedar swamps, bogs, marshes and springs. And it is teaming with brookies. They love this stuff, thriving in the cool headwaters and the upwelling springs. Swamps have a way of humbling and humiliating those who venture into them. I've bailed out from more than one pair of waders, leaving them stuck in a quagmire of mud and rotting vegetation. The trek back to the car is always longer when your tail is between your legs. Just for the record, there is no safe way to carry a fully rigged flyrod through a cedar swamp.

In the swamp, the mosquitoes look like they could be carrying malaria. As soon as you turn off the truck engine, they descend upon the cab. Boldly they taunt the foolish, those wearing "approved" bug repellents, to come outside. They do, however, have a healthy respect for the local bug juice. It's sold from under the counter in the town grocery store and farm supply outlet. There's no label on the bottle, but it's the only stuff that works. Applying it, you have the feeling that not even the boys in the military would test this stuff on their troops. A concoction of ingredients salvaged from a landfill site in the next township, each purchase comes with a verbal confidence-builder: "Don't worry, the burnin'll stop in about five minutes." Usually it does.

In the cool, clear headwaters, the brook trout were living up to their name: *Salvelinus* meaning "char" and *fontinalis*, "living in springs." Under normal conditions speckles are hard to catch. They are spooky. If pricked by a hook, they quickly learn and become more wary. A few loud footfalls or yells of "I'm stuck!" and they know something is up. They will hug the bottom and stop feeding. But not here in the boonies. Not here at the edge of the angling universe as we know it. Not in this inhospitable and inhumane swampland. In this watershed, they seldom feel a hook twice. The locals fish them with live bait. The concept of catch-and-release or fishing barbless, like the asphalt, has yet to reach these communities. "Out of the river and onto the barbie" should be the township motto. Most of the oldtimers think the possession limit for one day is "all you can carry."

Stephan christened these fish "hillbilly trout." These are ruffians. Uneducated and uncouth brookies. Seldom fished and unwise to the ways of the angler, they go after anything, often making three or four slashes at the same fly going down a drift. This is something an educated brookie would never do—and, outside of this watershed, unheard-of behavior. To prove it, Stephan developed and refined, but thankfully failed to get a patent on, the "Upstream Trolling Technique," and he was a master at it. Simply put: drag any surface pattern upstream and the "billies" would pounce on it. Until today, all we had to do was chuck in a fly and the billies would be in a panic over who was going to get to it first. We could break every law in the fly-presentation book and they would still take them. The trip was always a great ego boost. Not this time.

Usually we'd wander upstream, casting into riffles. The fish hang out there, seeking the extra oxygen being bubbled into the water. Stephan and I had gone through all the regular patterns: Black Gnats, Wee Muddlers, Big Joe's Boatmen, Smushed Hoppers, Kolking's Caddis, Scuds, Klinkhamer Specials and Mackerel Nymphs. They all struck out. Fortunately, the slower pools were filled with chub. These minnows attacked anything drifting past them, providing hot action during the slow periods when the speckles were off the feed.

From behind some tall Joe-pye weed came the gruff voice of Linda's father: "You boys catching any?"

"Naw," I said. "Pretty slow. Hardly had a hit."

"Diddly squat," added Stephan.

"You've been at it aw day. What ya usin'?" was the inquisitive reply. Thinking that "hydropsyche larva" might miss the mark, I went with "I've got on a small green bug and Stephan's using a small dry."

"Try an Edwards Post-OviPostin' Adult Caddis. Size 16 worked for me yesterday. Took fifteen fish in less than an hour. Let it hang at the end of the drift." I had to steady myself from rolling off the rock. Stephan quit in mid-cast. The caterpillars raised their heads, then quickly went back to eating. Obviously their silken sleeping bags were not far off. I stammered something like, "When'd you take up fly fishing?"

"Since I got fed up usin' chub tails 'n' too old 'n' lazy to dig worms."

I couldn't fault the logic.

"If ya need a brew, there's lots on the porch. You know where to find the good stuff. Take one with ya when ya go." Touched by the warmth of his kindness, I shouted, "Thanks," and reached for my fly box. Stephan was doing the same. "Keep in mind, now, that Caddis is a good low-water fly. Great when it's bright and sunny. See ya!"

Sending up a flurry of waxwings, I could hear

him busting through the cedars, his coon hounds scurrying around him. I just knew he was chuckling. Before we were out of earshot, he flippantly added, "If you city boys need some flies ... (*SNAP*) ... my vest's ... (*SNAP*) ... beside my ...

(*CRUNCH*) ... waders, hanging in the bank barn. Here, dog! Git over, ya silly dog!"

For a moment, through half a heartbeat, the wind carried my wake-up call and the aromatic smell of coffee.

River of Maternity

On the whole, women take to fly fishing faster than men do. They have an ability to get fish—big fish—when most men on the river have gone fishless. Even the most skilled and productive fishermen will freely admit that at some point they have had to take a back seat to the female gender. Why not? Nothing wrong with that, all's fair in love and ... you know.

There are hundreds of reasons why women hook more fish than men do, ranging from their nurturing abilities and sensitive nature to the fact that fish-repellant hormonal secretions are lower in females than in males. I'm convinced they take instruction better than men do, and they actually listen to what's being said. Combine these traits with their ability to know where things are and their highly developed observational skills, and it is easy to see the roots of their angling success.

Most guys in the brotherhood of the worldwide x y club, like myself, are products of the same male mold: "What did I do with the car keys? What does my wife of fifteen years take in her coffee? What was I supposed to pick up on the way home from work?" And the ever-popular, "Where *did* I leave the kids when I was ... ?"

Women, on the other hand, pay attention to the details and, it would seem, can effortlessly remember stuff. "Hey, Honey, seen the car keys?" Without glancing up from the newspaper: "On top of the fridge. Pick up some milk when you're out." They know where the keys are, and they know the milk-supply meter is showing "E."

"Any idea where I put my socket set?"

"Beside the paint cans in the garden shed. It's been there since you tuned up the lawn mower and busted it."

Most big fish are like UFOs—they show up when you are alone, in a secluded spot and have no witnesses. But when fishing with the fairer sex, I've discovered that the out-of-the-ordinary happens with extraordinary regularity. Over the years I have spent many hours on the water fishing with women, and these stories illustrate female fishing intuition at its best.

There was a little coffeehouse I used to frequent. It sold a great cup of coffee, served in hand-painted, locally fired mugs. Solid, heavy coffee mugs—the kind with a handle you could easily fit three or four fingers into if you felt the urge to do so. It sold *coffee*, none of that espresso, cappuccino, trendy, "gotta have a second language to order it" stuff. *Coffee*, that's what it said outside on the building sign and that's what they sold inside. That's why a whole bunch of folks hung out there, and, to soothe the nerves and feed my addiction, I'd stop in on the way home from the gym.

It was a quaint place—warm, cozy, friendly, with a handful of tables with tops of gray-flecked tiles, a scuffed-up wooden floor, and in one corner some big, comfy chairs. One wall was all window, framed with wide oak trim. It made it an ideal spot for a wee bit of people watching. A set of double doors formed the entrance. These, too, were framed in solid oak, and had smoked-glass centers, upon which entwining grapevines had been etched. The doors looked and felt historical, and the brass handles were well polished from years of use. The clientele was a mixed bunch, mostly in their mid-twenties to late-forties. It was a great meeting spot: students, professors and artsy types sporting body piercings—the "I'll show you mine if you show me yours, but you gotta show me first" group—same-sex couples and nostalgic folkies in designer purple peasant dresses (probably underwear coordinated), driving brand-new Volvo station wagons. In two years of going there, never once did I have a conversation with anyone about fly fishing until the day I showed up wearing one of my Rusty Rat brooches on my jacket.

I opened the door and walked into a wall of

sound. Beethoven's Symphony #5 in C minor, Op. 67 (*Allegro con brio*) almost blew me onto my butt and back out onto the sidewalk. Candy—affectionately called "Puss 'n' Boots"—was working behind the counter. We smiled at each other. "HELP YOURSELF! I'M MAKING MUFFINS." She motioned as if to turn down the music. I shook my head: "LEAVE IT! IT'S FINE!"

I poured myself a coffee, topped it off with cream, picked up a newspaper and wandered down the counter to pay her at the till. Beethoven was toned down by the time I got there, which was a little disappointing. Like it does a good AC/DC tune, the volume dial brings out the subtleties of the work and the rhythmical components often missed when it's played at the softer end of the decibel scale. Candy was tall, had an hourglass figure, and, depending on her mood, she'd wear a full-length dress with no makeup, and have a woman hanging on her arm. Or, if she felt like wearing a short leather skirt and a black, silver-studded dog collar with "Spike" engraved on the brass nameplate, a guy.

Today was different. Her bright green hair was up, her nose ring and tongue stud were in, and eight or nine gold hoops adorned each ear. She was draped in a well-oversized, just-above-the-knees, black cotton sweater, which stopped short of a pair of amazingly purple brushed-suede boots. Around her neck was a choker made from a length of barbed-wire. "Hey, that's a nice Rusty Rat. Who tied it?"

"Eeer … aaaa … I did. I tied it. That's what I do for a living; I tie flies, I teach folk how to fish and I make fly-fishing brooches. This one's a sample." She studied the fly more carefully, and obviously with an educated eye. "It's well balanced, but the wing is a bit on the thick side. You could never fish that—it will clump-up when it's swung through a pool on a deep drift. It'll take lots of current to move that. The body's nice 'n' flat, 'n' it's got a great hackle. Just give me a dollar and we'll call it even."

"Eeer … sure." Still slightly stunned, I paid her. "I didn't know you fly fished?"

"Yeah, had to. I grew up on the east coast, and

my dad used to guide and tie flies for some of the big lodges. When I left, I went up to a lodge near the Arctic and worked as a cook. Wanted to find myself."

"Did you?"

"Nah! I still wanted to be a classical pianist. Only thing I found out for sure was that it's as boring as hell pulling in grayling cast after cast after cast. They are pretty, but they can be a real nuisance." She pointed to the fly. "That's a small head you've got on that. Isn't it supposed to be red, not black?"

"Yeah, that's what the pattern books say. Mind now, it's for wearing not for fishing—that's why the wing's a bit thick, so it stands out on a lapel. When I'm at art shows, folks buy them as birthday gifts and stocking stuffers. The black head matches the hook. Anyway, most of the Rats I send out to the coast have black heads. The fish don't seem to mind."

She laughed, "No, but the sports do." Then she added: "Who made the blank pin? I've never seen a traditional salmon hook tied as a brooch."

"I did. I soldered on a clasp, then dressed the fly over the top." Reaching behind her neck she undid her necklace and handed it to me, "Can you fix this? I made it, but the clasp keeps breaking off." It felt warm. I caught a faint whiff of her Chanel and noticed a ring of little indentations around her throat. "I don't know. I'll try." The door opened and, just before she left to tend to her customers, she whispered, "Don't take too long with it. I feel kinda naked without it."

"Ho," I said in an understanding tone. Later, on the way out, I gave her my brooch, thinking, "It shows to go you."

Before she left on a scholarship to the States, eventually winding up going on to Europe, she fished with me on and off for several seasons. And could she fish! Her roll casts were exquisite, effortless and highly effective; on just about every trip, I watched her pull salmon, steelhead, bass and pike out of spots where unsuccessful fisherman—fly and spin fishermen—had been trying for hours. She had an uncanny knack for knowing *exactly* where a fish would be holding in a river. Lots of times we'd be walking on the bank, surveying a pool or a riffle, and I'd see nothing but boulders and bubbles. Then, in a very matter-of-fact way, she would say, "There's a fish in there. Can't you feel it?" I'd give her my blank, expressionless, "you're talking quantum physics" look. Sure enough, within a few casts there would be something finny leaping around on the end of her line.

Each trip started out the same way. I'd have to wait for her to arrive. She was always *exactly* five minutes late. The only time she wasn't late was when we snuck into an auditorium in the wee hours of a January morning. I sat in the front row, as Spike, in total darkness, played Beethoven's Moonlight Sonata—my all-time favorite chunk of music—as a birthday present.

I never knew what she'd be wearing when she showed up for a fishing trip or what her hair color would be, but the one thing I was always sure of was her ability to cast a fly and hook fish. On the water, she turned lots of heads, and not because of what she was—or sometimes wasn't—wearing.

"Take me with you tomorrow when you go steel-heading?"

"What?"

"I'd like to go get a steelhead."

"What are you up to?"

"Nothing. I wouldn't mind going."

"I don't know, lass, it's a loogan-fest up there. Wall to wall yahoos. I'm not being sexist, but it's hardly the place for a woman. It's a bunch of drunks making fools of themselves, snagging fish. Last time I was up there, I almost got into a fist fight, and the time before that I did. It's like the wild west." I looked her up and down, "At five-two and 120 pounds, you'll hardly be able to hold your own."

She smiled, threw her arms around my neck and planted a kiss. "You forgot to say: successful, blond, intelligent and damn cute."

I let out a long, slow sigh. "Yi'll no get an argument from me on that, lass, but you forgot to add funny, warm and mischievous."

"Mischievous? Me? Oh no, no, no. *You* don't understand women."

"Ho. I think I understand them well enough, and just as much as I want to."

"I'll go pack my ski clothing. Besides, I'll keep you company on the drive." She wandered off to find her jacket, and I packed another couple of rods and her waders into the car.

In the early 1980s much of Southern Ontario was gripped with salmon and steelhead fever. Many of the fingerling stockings dumped into the waters of the Great Lakes were now "all growed up" and starting to run the rivers as spawning adults. And there was a madness on these rivers. Catch-and-release was almost unheard of, possession limits were high and mob rule was in many places—especially in the wee hours of the morning—the order of the day. Many a time I'd seen the banks turn red with the blood of slaughtered fish. During these dark ages—in a time before *that* Robert Redford movie—fly fishermen were regarded by most of the angling brotherhood as a pain in the ass, some may say we still are, and they had very strong opinions about women having no place on the river. There were perhaps a few dozen fly fisherman dookin' it

out in the madness, blazing a trail, and making it safe for those who now follow in designer fly-fishing clothing, driving airconditioned fly-fishing-edition sport utility vehicles—complete with compact-disk players and heated leather seats.

Fly fishermen were not tolerated on the river. Going along the bank I'd hear comments like, "You're gonna scare the fish using a line like that." They would deliberately tangle up my gear or wade through the center of the pool I was fishing. Usually I managed to eke out a spot by confronting the lads, using a thick Scottish accent. When your best defense is a good offense, comments like, "Hey pal! It's awfully cold tae be goin' swimmin'" would get me some space. If it didn't, I'd bounce a few back casts off jackets, hoods and baseball caps. Only once did I have to drive the fly into the back of someone's neck to get the point across. "Ho. Sorry, pal! Didn't see ya back there ... Mind if I get that back? ... It's the last number-2 Zonker I have. It's barbless; it should fall straight oot! ... Ho, it's no barbless?— well, silly me! ... Ho, well, you might want to get that looked at by a doctor ... I think the hook might be wee bit on the rusty side ... Don't worry about the fly, just keep it!"

Into this Kingdom of Freakdom, I was taking a novice fly fisherman. Granted she'd done well over the summer, catching bass, and she had a flare for hooking big fish that everyone else had missed. So, on the two-hour drive north to the river, I was thinking to myself—as she slept in the passenger seat—"It might work out okay." At six a.m., awash in the glow from a burning garbage can, I pulled into a packed parking lot, thinking "Here we go!" and woke up Sparkles.

Under the acrid and pungent stench of burning plastic, we climbed into our waders. I assembled the gear and we set off toward the river down a well-worn trail, cunningly marked with cigarette packages, paper coffee cups, empty pop and beer cans, into a small grove of trees. Through the bare winter branches, we could see the dancing bonfire flames, and when we cleared the treeline the scene before us could have inspired Dante.

With their backs toward us, the lads were lined up shoulder to shoulder along the edge of the river. From the head of the line, 25 yards upstream, to the right, was the base of a dam. Legally, no fishing was allowed in that section of water, although the boys were casting into it. The downstream end of the chain-gang stopped at the top edge of a fast set of rapids. Here, like a beacon warning of the dangers downstream, the fire was blazing away on the bank, surrounded by a couple of busted deck chairs and several open cases of beer. On top of the fire were the blackened remains of deck-chair frames, sitting like a giant spider, waiting patiently for unwary fishermen.

The edge of the river was packed, and there were more fisherman than you could shake a stick at. Sparkles looked at me. "Where are we gonna fish?"

"Ho, give me a minute, lass, I'll think of something." She looked at the river, then looked at me. "What's your best informed opinion?" she chuckled, knowing full well I hadn't one.

My guess was that the lads were trying to snag fish in the slow pool directly in front of them. As the light from the dam drifted downstream, bathing the scene in a filter of black and white, the light echoed the space around it, and only harsh, sharp edges danced across the hinterland. I called it, pointing to the tail end of the line. "Let's try between that last guy and the fire."

"Can't we try away down there, where no one's fishing?" she asked hesitantly, pointing into a spot some 300 yards downriver.

"We could, but there's always a fish or two hanging out in that pocket between tail-end Charlie and the big rock just downstream of the blaze. No point in wandering all the way down there. There are fish here. That's our best shot."

En route to taking up our positions and merging with the mob, we passed the corpses of several female salmon, their bellies slit open and eggs removed. They were large empty envelopes, left to litter the stones as gull food. Five-gallon, white plastic buckets were dotted among the anglers, so it wasn't a far stretch of the imagination to figure out where the roe had gone, gathered for steelhead bait.

I stood beside the last downstream guy in the line; Sparkles was two steps below me, to my left. After snagging the chap's float several times, my saber-rattling was successful, and eventually he stopped drifting his float down into the water we were fishing. Out went her line, and a size-6 Zulu disappeared into the blackness. Fourth cast in, just at the end of her drift, in the cushion of water in front of the boulder, her line tightened. A bright silver shape started cartwheeling and porpoising across the top of the water. Even in the dull light from the fire, the shape was unmistakable; she had hooked a very large steelhead, and, once again, in the space of forty-five minutes I was thinking, "Here we go." Her rod started thumping, and she looked at me with a terrible grin and a gleam in her eyes, brighter than the trail of fire-sparks dancing and spiraling skyward. I'd seen it before and knew it could only mean one thing. As all heads turned to see who had the fish on, Sparkles shouted at the top of her lungs, "FISH! I'VE A BIG FISH ON. SOMEBODY GET ME A NET!" Never before had she requested such an item.

Nervously, I smiled at her, rolled my eyes, thought, "Oh boy!" and quietly said to her, "That's a very big steelhead you've got on." Instantaneously, as if continuing my sentence, "GET YOUR LINES IN. BIG RAINBOW COMIN' UP!" erupted from somewhere deep within a small blue ski jacket. The angling responses to a tremendous explosion of excited emotion like hers can differ strongly. Either lines are obligingly pulled in, or, more than likely, the statement is the leading edge of an angry altercation. Betting on the latter, I mentally prepared for a quick round of boxing and some "full-contact fly fishing."

"BIG FISH COMIN' UP!" By now, three or four guys had formed a netting posse, and along the length of the pool most of the lads were reeling in lines. She looked at me with a widening grin, then started hollering at one fisherman who still had his line in the water. "Hey! I've a big 'bow on here, get your bloody line out the water!" This, from a woman whom I'd never heard raise her voice. Shooting stars danced in her pupils, and without question she now had center stage. I'd seen those sparkles before, and I was having a very bad feeling.

The fish was going ballistic. Tail-walking. Cartwheeling. Long reel-busting runs. Vicious head shakes. This was in the good old days, before hatchery stockings had watered down the gene pool, and, unlike those we catch now, this fish fought like a demon. Sparkles had pulled off her touque and fluffed out her hair. There was little doubt that a *woman* was attached to the rod. The mumblings and rumblings of the crowd were getting louder. There were now six guys holding nets, *all* eager to oblige if required. She was letting out gasps and yells I'd heard only in our most intimate of moments.

"Oh! Just great!" I muttered under my breath, amazed at the incredible amount of effort she was using to prevent herself from exploding with laughter.

The fish was making one last run. She looked straight into my eyes and hollered, "HO! ... Ohhhhh!" Her cry echoed across the river, and was lost to the swift-flowing riffles. "HO ... MY ... GOD!" was added, seconds later, just for effect. Stripping in line, the fish slipped within landing range, and a ruck of hopeful anglers thrust nets toward the boils and swirls in the shallow water. Luckily, in the ensuing melee, the fish found a net—probably looking for some type of cover to avoid serious bodily injury—and, as it was hoisted into the air, she winked and grinned at me, then headed off to claim her prize. I glanced around the river. No one was fishing. She had cleared out the pool.

Lifting the fish from the net, the fly dropped free from the hinge of its jaw. It looked like a bar of pure silver, a beautiful male fish with a cherry-red stripe running along the length of its body, tipping the scales at around 12 pounds.

The firelight flickered across the shimmering skin, making the fish glow and seem ephemeral. There were "Ooohs" and "Ahhhas," from the throng, who were working under the assumption that the fish was destined to be dispatched, boinked on the head, whacked into the next dimension—bound for a plastic-wrap shroud and a humming white crypt in a basement. These aspirations were snuffed out when she knelt down and slipped the fish beneath the inky surface, releasing it back into the night. She stood up and addressed her audience, saying, "I just don't see what all the fuss is about." Knowing exactly when to quit, she added, "Let's go and get breakfast."

"Yi'll no get an argument from me on that, lass."

Slogging through a brisk fall day on a trout river without a hit is a disappointment. Slogging through a brisk fall day on a trout river without a hit, guiding a client who won't listen to instruction and who has a blatant disregard for warnings about treacherous water, is nothing short of a nightmare. Several times I'd looked up to the heavens, asking "Ho, God, send me a lawyer."

The appropriate action is to cancel the lesson and leave the chap in the river. However, when his *partner* has left him stranded by driving off in the Beamer, other than administering a good drowning—not a great idea, as the insurance rates would go through the roof—the only option is sticking it out. So I did. Now, those of you who are not in the guiding profession—with all due respect, I'm not talking about cookies and camp-fires—may find my reference to this method of dealing with the client a wee bit on the strong side. You'll just have to trust me on this. I've yet to meet a guide who has enjoyed dealing with one of these armchair anglers who learned to fly fish from watching fishing shows on TV, and now knows *all* about it. *Arrrrrrggghhhh!* Little wonder I've lost most of my hair.

The day was drawing to a close, and the river was in a state of turmoil, switching the biomass clocks over from daylight feeding time to night-light feeding time. Mr. Happy, my client, and I stood on a high bridge above the river, waiting for Gina to arrive with the BMW. Gina, Mr. Happy's *friend* from the office, was almost five-foot-three—in heels—and about 105 pounds. She had dark brown eyes, shoulder-length jet-black hair, and her olive skin was a dead giveaway that she had Polynesian roots. The last we saw of her,

she was wearing a short suede skirt, black stock-ings and a mid-length mink jacket. She'd slipped behind the wheel of the BMW, spun the tires, laid down a good yard of rubber, dissolving in a shower of roadside dust and gravel, and headed toward town.

Looking down from the bridge, it was too easy to see the best holding water and the best pools. Of course, we'd seen these spots up close and personal, as we had fished every one of them, *several times*, throughout the day. The river surface was fragmented with large white boulders and freckled with feeding fish. There were splashy rises, gentle sips, small bulges; pick a rise form and they were doing it. Looking at the river, I was thinking that "nothing lives in isolation." The number of fish was almost beyond contemplation, and our lack of success was nothing short of remarkable.

Gina popped out of the car and asked how our day had been. Grumbling beside the open trunk, waders were getting removed and there was much cursing and swearing. I was looking down at the water. Gina joined me as the grumblings from the back of the Beamer became louder. Halfway through explaining to her how the river system worked, she shouted to the back of the car, "How come you didn't get any? There's so many fish. It sounds easy."

"Well, if it's that easy, why the hell don't you try it?"

"Fine! I will! I've got a license you know!" She picked up his rod and looked at me. Meanwhile, I'm thinking, "When did I sign up?" then, as I am prone to do, I opened my mouth before my brain was fully functioning. "Right, then, let's have a go at it." He slammed down the trunk and wandered over to the side of the bridge to watch.

Fashion footwear was never designed to be worn on the steep embankments leading down to river-access points. Gina was doing a heck of a job, gingerly picking her way around the large stones and the plant roots. She made it to the bottom without slipping, then I realized the flaw in my plan. The water in front of us was only knee deep at best, and the fish were out nearer

the middle of the river, quite accessible if you were wearing waders, which she was not. I could wet-wade in bare feet and give her the use of mine, but they would be way too big, and therefore dangerous. Asking Mr. Happy if we could borrow his waders did not seem like a wise choice. I looked at Gina. "We need to get out to the other side of the boulders."

"So take me."

"What?"

"Take me." Until she said it, the thought of carrying her out there had never occurred to me. Actually, since I'd made the commitment up on the bridge nothing much had occurred to me. She stood on a small boulder and kicked off her heels into the grass. "Right! Fair enough!" Confidence hid my strong feelings of pending disaster. Worst thing that could happen—we'd both get a soaker.

I knelt down and slung her up over my shoulder, saying "Whatever you do, don't move." I had no idea why I said that, but it seemed like the thing to say. Like John the Baptist, I waded out to the first boulder and placed her down on it. Some-times a guide's gotta do what a guide's gotta do.

Not once did Gina turn around and look to the bridge. To avoid spooking the fish, she worked at throwing cast after cast into the area we had just waded through, and I worked at keeping her on top of the boulder. Ten minutes passed and she graduated from practising to fishing by flipping a size-8 Feeble Freestone nymph into the faster water, out toward the center of the river. The nymph, the pattern that Mr. Happy had been using, was drifting down through the same current breaks he had been fishing.

During her third or fourth pass, she could detect tapping on her line. "Those little tap-tap-taps are chub. They sit in the slow spots," I said. Pointing to some quicker water, I added, "Try getting the fly out a wee bit further, into the fast bubbly stuff." She did.

We had a few false alarms when she tapped out on rocks and weeds, then the inevitable happened. One of the boulders started running downstream and across the current. After a brief two- or three-minute tussle, I slipped my hand around the fat tummy of a 2-pound brown trout. Gina seemed less than impressed by the fish. I removed the fly and offered her the fish. "Want to hold it and I'll get a few photos?" "Hell, NO! All I wanted to do was hook one. Let it go. I don't want to get slime on my jacket. But make sure *he* gets a good look at it before you let it go." I did. Sometimes a guide's gotta do ...

At some point in her life, Sue, an Aquarius, was anointed and blessed by the fish gods—all of them. She was a highly successful businesswoman, starting and building a company from the ground up into a national corporation. Representing Canada on trade missions, she has a feisty, no-nonsense, don't-screw-with-me attitude toward business. "Don't tell me you're gonna do it. Get it done!" would be the perfect bumper-sticker for this lady.

She gave herself a set of fly-fishing lessons as a retirement present. Her exact words were: "Listen, Ian, I'm selling my business next Thursday and

I'm taking up fishing on Friday." On the Tuesday I called to confirm things with her. We'd go for pike and bass near our *alma mater*, the University of Guelph. On Friday morning she showed up at exactly eight o'clock. We'd begun getting on the gear when her cell phone started ringing. She checked the number and tossed it in the trunk of her car, saying, "Screw 'em. I'm retired."

Sue, as I said, was blessed by the fish gods. Over the summers I've watched her haul fish out of areas where there should be none. Her special talent for catching big fish from impossible places first surfaced on a steamy summer day. The weather was hot and humid, around 38 degrees Centigrade, and the July sun shone relentlessly from a cloudless blue sky. Seeking refuge from the heat—and from a morning of successful smallmouth-bass fishing—we plopped ourselves into the middle of a trout creek to work on some of her dry-fly presentations.

The canopy of trees from both banks hung out over the river, almost touching each other. Looking up, the sky was a scribble of blue crayon between the tree tops. Sue had on a size-8 Double Elk Hair Caddis on 10 feet of 8-pound leader, the same setup she'd been using for bass earlier in the day. On her third drift past a semi-submerged cedar log, the fly disappeared in a swirl no larger than a raindrop would make hitting the surface. Minutes later, she was holding a beautiful 2-pound speckled trout. Until her fish showed up, the largest speckled trout taken from this river was just under a pound, with the larger ones being caught when the water was cool, just before the season closed in the fall.

One hot, sticky summer afternoon, Sue put on one of the most incredible fish-catching clinics I have ever witnessed, and she set a benchmark that will probably never be surpassed. The sky was cloudless, with lax leaves hanging on the solid walls of willows lining the riverbanks. The river was low, slow moving and choked with weeds— masses of long, dark green tentacles flowing in the currents, like long hair floating in a bathtub. To find the best fish-holding pockets, a bit of aerial reconnaissance is required, and when I viewed it from the treetop branches the water was a seething mass of moss-colored jellyfish.

The only way to tackle these fish was to use small surface patterns, drifting them down the foot-wide gaps in the weeds. Sue threw out a 30-foot cast and the size-8 Double Elk Hair Caddis skipped across the surface. There was a huge boil. She lifted into the fish, and it went nuts. In the weeds, out the weeds, runs downstream, runs upstream—it was doing it all. Eventually I waded into the weeds, and, when she swung the fish past the edge, I grabbed it. An 18-inch smallmouth.

"That's a beautiful fish. I've never seen one that big in here. Biggest I've got is a 12. You're lucky, take a good look at it, you might never see another one like it." We admired the fish then released it, and I asked if she wanted the fly snipped off to keep as a memento. "It's working. Let's keep fishing it." I greased it up, we wandered 3 feet downstream, and she pitched out the fly. On this cast she landed a 13-incher, on her next a 16, followed by, on consecutive drifts, an 11 and a 15. There is, I feel, nothing left to say.

The bass season was almost two weeks old when Cathy called and asked if I would help her to try her hand at fly fishing. She was planning ahead: her new job was taking her up north, into the heart of some of the best fishing in Ontario, to the top west pocket of the province, along the leading edge of Lake Superior, to cities like Sault Ste. Marie, Fort Frances and Thunder Bay.

Cathy is brilliant. She is one of those gifted people who has the ability to pick things up after one or two pointers, a great listener who cuts through the bull and gets to the guts of the matter by asking just the right questions at just the right time. Plus, she's the only woman I know who has lost a mitten throwing snowballs at an iceberg and who has hunted caribou—successfully—with the Inuit. Drop Cathy in the bush with a rusty pocketknife and she'd have a birchbark canoe made in no time. Having made it, she'd be in her element, cutting through dangerous white water with nothing more than an old, trusted-but-busted paddle.

We arrived at the fishing spot just as the sun was burning off the morning mist, and climbed into our waders. For gear there was nothing too serious: 6-weight rods with double tapered floating lines and a box packed full of Mugwumps, Dexters and Buzbys. Most of the river was slow moving, no more than a foot deep, low and clear, with the occasional pocket falling down to about 4 feet. The banks were thick with purple loostrife and alive with the murmurings of insects. A perfect morning to learn to fly-fish.

Within the fly-fishing fraternity, this river has become *the place* to be seen in Southern Ontario. Fortunately, most of these folk are "bridgers"; they gear up, fish within a hundred yards of the nearest bridge or access point, then drive home convincing themselves they just had a wilderness experience. Nothing wrong with that, but it makes for some awfully crowded spots on the river.

From the bridge, this section looks like dead water. The rolls of discarded fencing wire and the partially silted-in tires littering the riverbed don't do much for the ambiance, but upstream, out of sight of the bridge, it's another world. Carp—big carp, big beautiful carp, the "Queen of the Water," as Izaak Walton called them, or as I prefer to call them "Ol' Yeller"—cruise the shallows like golden pot-bellied pigs. Then there are pike, rainbows, cute little stocked brown trout, suckers, smallmouth and rock bass, all calling this section of the river home and all willing to take a fly.

A "plague of porcupines" populates these riverbanks, which I figure is better than an "enigma of fly fishers." When the fishing is slow, watching porcupines doing what porcupines do—mostly sitting in trees or eating—always lightens the heart. Porcupines have a "So what?" attitude, and could best be described as Canadian sloths. When they amble—they have only two speeds, amble and stop—along a trail, the tinkling and rustling of their quills sounds like a million tiny wind chimes.

Slowly moving down the center of the river, Cathy was hooking—Let's try that again. Slowly moving down the center of the river, Cathy had mastered the roll cast and was taking fish after fish, mostly rock bass, and, for a bit of variety, an occasional smallmouth. Without a fly, I'd roll-cast my line across a pocket or a set of riffles. Cathy would make the same cast—the only difference being that she had a size-6 Mugwump on the end of her leader. There would be a boil beneath the surface and she'd lift into a fish.

Here, in the fall, using a Big Joe's Crayfish or a surface Cranefly, I'd land oodles of smallmouth in the 10-inch range. If I was lucky, I'd get one or two 12-inch fish just before the season closed, when, sensing the onset of winter, the bass would make pigs of themselves, greedily packing on extra weight. Although Cathy and I had spooked dozens of crayfish, watching them scoot for cover between the fist-sized pebbles, minnow-type patterns always did well for the first half of the season, and the Mugwump she was using was getting the snot well and truly kicked out of it. We watched a few carp tailing in the shallows, only to have them disappear in puffs of mud when she threw the fly at them.

By the time we rounded a sharp bend in the river, 400 yards upstream of the bridge, the sun had chased away most of the shadows, bleaching out the rich morning hues and warm tones. There was a fast set of riffles in the middle of the river, and, as it curved to the left there was a delicious-looking pocket along the inside edge. Cathy was trying to explain the subtleties of canoeing in such a spot, when her line tightened up. There was not much in the way of a boil; it was tough to see the hit, as it was just at the edge of the fast water. She set the hook and the fish started peeling line from the reel. As there were no violent head shakes, I figured she was into a carp.

It was a decent fish, hugging the bottom and keeping a good bend in the rod. Minutes later, she pushed the tip of her rod into the air and as the fish swung into the shallows, I lip-landed a 15-inch smallmouth and handed it to her. It looked like a rugby ball—plump in the middle and streamlined at the ends. I didn't know who was more surprised—Cathy, the bass or me. She released it and then decided she'd had enough for the day. Once again, the expert was suffering from the heavy blows of fate. Before she landed *that* fish,

I always figured 10 inches was a decent size. I've spent days fishing the same pocket, and over the years I have never been able to hook a bass larger than 13 1/2 inches.

Opening Day

The calendar unfolded as it should, sending the last Saturday of April up to bat. The opening day of trout season shot over the plate, riding a wicked curve ball. Across Ontario, thousands of fishermen donned their gear and courageously stepped onto the playing field. With unseasonably low temperatures, near-flood conditions and a falling barometric pressure, the weather showed no mercy. It hit a home run out of the park. Many of the faithful didn't make it out of the batting cage. Game over.

It's different for me. I'm a guide. A fly-fishing instructor. It's my job to coach my clients around the bases. Regardless of the odds, they have to feel their cleats sliding safely across home plate before the day is over. Every trip's a "Field of Dreams." I take their fantasies and help fulfill them. The perfect haul. A drag-free drift. The magical back-lit cast in the glowing embers of a sunset. Over the years I've been privileged to watch many of them hook and land their first fish on a flyrod. They've done it all, and I've been beside them, whispering words of support and encouragement.

But not today. This is opening day, and aquatic insanity reigns supreme.

For reasons that will soon become clear, I seldom fish the opener. If I do, it is never with a client. It would be with one of a handful of close friends whose willingness to laugh outweighs their lust or desire to catch a fish. And I was about to do just that.

All winter long the glossy fishing magazines have dropped through the nation's mail slots. In these slick, four-color pages, fantasy and reality meld in each closeup, touched-up photo of fish and fly. More than expectations are raised. Now those well-thumbed, dogeared pages, read only for the articles and editorials, have been slipped back under the bed. It's here. Opening day, and school's out for the summer. Equipment purchased from the midwinter magazine ads begins to appear. Promising to make fishing trips more pleasurable, the stuff sprouts like wild spring crocuses along the riverbank. The cost per fish in must-have gear goes through the roof. A second mortgage may be required. Opening day brings it all out of the closet and into the harsh light of the fishing world. It is seldom pleasant, often a frenzied fly-fishing free-for-all.

During the first weekend of the season, the river resembles a very bad Santa Claus parade or a Mardi Gras nightmare. The new gear. The colorful, trendy clothing. All of the Fishing Christmas Gifts are dragged out of the closet and put on with zealous anticipation. Then it's down to the Swanee River. But that's all right—it is, after all, the opener. There are fish to catch, and catch them fly-fishers will.

As for the fish. Since the season closed some seven months ago, the fish have been relatively undisturbed, living, one would assume, placid, peaceful lives. Chasing a few bugs, spawning over perfectly dug-out gravel beds, and going about their fishy business in a relaxed and stress-free environment. All that's about to change.

To coin a phrase: "They're all spooked to rat shit." Now, I have personally never seen scared-rat droppings. But, what I have seen are opening-day rivers where the fish would gladly head to the nearest war zone for some peace and quiet. Nothing will put fish "down" and "off the feed" quicker than a herd of nomadic anglers stumbling down a river. It's not the splashing of these eager Bedouin that scares them. No, no—it's the gleeful yells of encouragement to fellow anglers that send fish scurrying long before they get to see a fishing fly or a pair of waders.

"You getting anything?" Not now.

"What are you using?" A flyrod.

"Any hits?" Nah, but stick around and you might get one or two.

"Try a small Adams." Why? Why in the name of God would I want to try a dry fly when today, like many an opening day before, the river looks like a ribbon of chocolate milk? I can't see my fingers 4 inches below the surface. There's a better chance of lobbing a brick from an orbiting space station and hitting one of the pyramids at Giza, than a fish seeing a dry fly under these conditions. I've found that, in these situations, it is best to work under the assumption that the town crier with the fishing pole has forgotten to take his medication before leaving the house. Wave in acknowledgment and mentally give him the sympathy vote. Do not, under any circumstances, engage in conversation. If you do, he will follow you up and down the river like a lost puppy, hand you his phone number, then invite himself over to your house for tea.

Having started out at three a.m., our two-hour car drive was decidedly uneventful. We had the age-old debate about the correct order to add vegetables into a stir-fry—Paul's a mushrooms-in-with-the-onions guy, and I take a mushrooms-in-with-the-red-peppers stance. It's one of those things we will never resolve, so we agree to disagree. Cocooned in the warm womb from the dashboard heater, we hurtled north, toward the fishing grounds. Outside, in the blackness, the wind howled. Loudly. We were soothed by the glow from the instrument panel. The headlights lit up the raindrops. I was convinced that I saw a few snowflakes trying to hide themselves among the shimmering comets splattering against the windscreen. No amount of persuasion from Paul could make me believe otherwise. He gripped the wheel as we talked of where to go and what to use. The middle section of the Maitland River won out on a split decision over the upper Saugeen River. Less fishing pressure, a greater area to fish and, we'd hoped, water with more visibility than a London fog tipped the hat in its favor.

Underneath our agreements and brave bravado we both knew the decision was still a crapshoot, and dodgy at best. I was not fully convinced about the venue. Paul is "a local" to these watersheds so, when in Rome ... I sat back and enjoyed the ride. Much sooner than I would have liked, we arrived. Opening the door, I stepped into the eerie, inhospitable predawn. I shuddered. It felt like summer in the Scottish Highlands. I felt suddenly homesick, remembering boyhood fishing days. Mini piles of snow had formed at the edge of the grass. Leaving the snug interior of the car, I saw the clock in the dash flashing 5:05. Christ. Now I know how Neil Armstrong felt with "One small step." I think I'd rather be sexing baby chickens.

I want my bed and a nice down comforter, with big fluffy pillows. I want to assume the fetal position with my lover. I need to feel skin—her skin—soft and warm beneath my forearm as I snuggle into her. I need to taste her perfume. I need to feel her long blond hair against me, listen to her gently breathing—breathing's good—as the rain gives the outside of the bedroom window a "right good beating." I *need* to get my equipment out of the trunk and get down to the river.

The open trunk illuminated the area like a nativity scene, and I was half-expecting three guys on camels to step out of the darkness, bearing gifts. Paul, a.k.a. "There's no way those are snowflakes,"

stepped out of the blackness. He, too, had seen the snow. Materializing from the far side of the car, he wore a sheepish grin. We put our waders on in silence. Draining the last of the extra large coffee from the take-out cup, I flipped the empty back into the trunk. Unlike my ears, the paper cup felt slightly warm. Paul's voice broke the silence. "Hey, pull the tab off that and see if you've won a prize." The coffee shop was running a promotion, offering prizes that included minivans, barbecues, free coffees, donuts and cookies. I did. I hadn't.

"I've never even won a free coffee," I said assembling my rod, line and leader.

"Don't worry. I've only won a cookie. Last year a guy I know won a TV." I was touched by the genuine warmth and condolence in his voice. I felt momentarily moved by his kind words. It's hard to tell when Paul is setting me up for something. Figuring his comment might be a small part of a bigger conspiracy, I asked if he was ready. I should have looked before I leaped. He was ready, but for what I wasn't sure. He'd somehow managed to squeeze into a pair of neoprene waders.

Neoprene—the same elastic material used in scuba-suit construction. With his 240 pounds of stock investor's lunches, he looked like a beached seal in a pair of thick green leotards. I raised my eyebrows, giving him a quizzical look.

"The wifie got me these for Christmas."

"She's got some sense of humor, does your Bronwyn. That lassie's right on top of things." I could see the photo on the front of the greeting card with the caption "When ballet dancers let themselves slide" printed underneath it.

This indeed was a Hallmark Moment, but I thought it best to avoid the subject.

Wriggling into his new fishing vest, beaming with pride, he held open the sides. "Taa-daa." With a curtsy he went into "sensitive" fashion-show-host mode.

"I see, Mr. James, you've chosen quite a sporty outfit for today's festivities. Would you like to tell the folks at home a little more about it?"

"Indeed. It's a cheeky little number. Something with a delicate touch and the ability to smash line into the teeth of a hurricane."

"Hah, would that be the 'pig rod' you're holding, Mr. James, the 'beast' that put the 20-yard roll cast within the reach of mere mortals? And, if I may say so, the little black dress of the fly-fishing world?"

"Aye, right enough, the 9-weight Iron Feather. For accessories I've gone with a double-tapered, size-10 floating line in a pastel peach. Finishing the outfit, in a delightful shade of anodized black, is a matching saltwater reel holding 290 yards of backing. The outfit can easily be dressed up for formal occasions or made into something more casual for just hanging out at the beach."

"An excellent choice, if I may say so."

"Thank you."

"Will you be taking prisoners today, Mr. James?"

"Nae chance."

"Well, folks, there you have it. It's big, it's mean, it's fly fishing like you've never seen. We will be right back after these messages, so hit the kitchen, grab a diet pop and put a party pizza in the oven. Today's show is gonna be a cracker!"

Paul reached up to close the trunk. "Hold it. You've got the keys. Right?" There was more concern in my voice than question.

"Yeah, in my jacket pocket."

"No, Paul. I mean you can *feel* them. Check and make sure before you close that. Remember Kirkland."

Letting go, he fumbled through his pockets. Kirkland. How could anyone forget it? I'd tried. Some nights it gripped me like a crocodile in a death roll. An hour down a bumpy, pothole-infested logging road. Peppering the roadside ditches were snowdrifts higher than a bear's arse. Kirkland, where the trout are all over 2 pounds. Kirkland, in a minus-10-degree windchill. Kirkland, where two guys were taking turns at lying in the open trunk of a two-week-old car, kicking in the back seat, then crawling through the opening into the passenger compartment. Our mission, which we had no choice *but* to accept: To rescue the car keys from his jacket pocket. Safely locked inside, they were on the floor below the driver's seat.

It took his wife over a year before she let him use the car again for fishing trips, and Paul six months to get over my bear comment. I discovered the keys locked inside the car and, with my nose still pressed against the window, said, "Hey, at least the bears won't be able to steal the stereo when we're fishing." Thinking back, it might have been my phrases uttered from inside the trunk that pushed him to the edge. Things like: "Hey, this *is* very spacious, just like the ads say ..." (*BOOT!*) "Don't ya just love the smell of a new car ..." (*BOOT!*) And as the bolts were pulling out of the back panel, ripping out chunks of padding with them, "Boy, I gotta tell ya, Paul, these things are awfully well put together ..." (*SPROING!*) The Kirkland Incident, as we had affectionately called it, was never spoken about in public. It was our Roswell.

"I've got my fingers on them," he said. With a click, the trunk closed. The light went out, dragging the temperature down with it.

I was slowly becoming accustomed to the dark as we started down the last of the road. "Looks like we're the only ones here, except for the minivan beside the cedars," Paul commented. "You could be right," I said, crossing my fingers. Please let him be right. "If ever there was a time for him to be right, let it be now," I mumbled under my breath to no one in particular. We walked toward the river. "Hey, this neoprene hardly makes a sound when my legs rub together." He was bringing the new waders up again. I wanted to nip it in the bud, or it would be all I'd hear about for the rest of the day.

"Yeah, this nylon makes a big racket." Until he had brought it up, I'd never noticed it before. Now, it was beginning to bother me. I was starting to suffer from quiet-crotch envy.

"Hey, these would be great to wear for sneaking up on things."

"Sure, Paul. And, just what *were* you planning to sneak up on?" I gave him the universal "You're a clown" look, ending it. Above the gloating confident swish, swish, swish of my waders, we could hear the river.

Rounding a bend in the trail, it was now "not snowing" a lot harder. In the gray twilight of morning, a hunched figure approached. Through the sleet. Through the *driving* sleet. As the troll-like shape drew nearer, we realized it was a very soggy angler with a very busted fishing pole. We said nothing, the distance between us growing shorter. Although tempting, this was hardly the time to inquire how his day was going. He walked despondently and was shrouded in an aura of complete failure and disillusionment. It spoke volumes. Having witnessed this many times before, we knew that the utmost discretion was required. In passing, he spoke only six words: "The rocks are kind of slippy."

We acknowledged him with a solemn head nod and passed in silence. "Been there, done that, got the T-shirt" was Paul's comment when we were further down the trail and out of earshot.

"Yeah! Me too," I replied, loudly swishing away.

"I'll bet that jacket would be toasty-warm if it were dry," he said with silent steps.

"Ho, no doubt. Probably wind-proof too. It looked expensive," I added.

"Christmas. From the wife and kiddies?"

"Absolutely, but he sure picked a hell of a day to test it out. I can see the bairns howling when he gets home. 'WHAAAA! Daddy got the jacket wet!'" Our laughter was riding high above the wind and the sound of my waders. We were in stitches. It stopped, abruptly, when we rounded the last bend in the trail and we got our first look at the river.

Neither of us was prepared for what we saw. It looked like something out of Edvard Grieg's *The Hall of the Mountain King*.

"How many guys can you get in a minivan?" I asked as the scene unfolded.

"Too many," was the reply.

The pool in front of us was packed. A quick head count gave the official attendance figure at twelve, that included Soggy the troll, who was heading back to the van. Fly-fishing trips are a continuous case of finding solutions to a litany of unanswered questions, and, right now, Paul and I needed answers to a whole bunch of them. Paul scanned the top section of the pack for signs of fish and signs of intelligent life, and I looked over the lower section. Nothing. No dead fish on the bank and no signs of a landing net. As for intelligent life, the jury was still out. If they had been catching fish, the net would have been in a prominent position, poised for instant use. Still looking things over, I mumbled to Paul, "How the hell did *this* lot find out about *this* spot. Nobody fishes here!"

"They do now. Don't worry, looks like they're struggling."

"True enough, but they are here. I'm asking." With those words I wandered into the thicket of anglers and gleefully inquired, "Hey guys. Gettin' any?"

"Nah, nothing. We've only had one fish on." Someone added, "It looked like a salmon." I glanced at Paul, raised my eyebrows, and having gone through this a million times, he picked up on it. We both knew this was a time for high-level diplomacy. "Yeah, could be. The guys down at the mouth were getting a bunch of those. That's why we left. We don't have the gear for big fish"—I tried to hide my monster pole—"We've never been up this far, took a wrong turn and followed the road till we got here. Thought it might cross back over. Saw your van and figured there must be fish in here."

"We've never fished here before, either. Saw it posted on the Internet." The leader of the pack had just told us what we wanted to know. I thought to myself, "The golden age is now long gone," and said, inquisitively, "The Internet?"

"Yeah, the guy's Web page said it was a great place to fish. It even had a map."

"Yeah, well, if it's that great, how come the guy who posted it ain't here?" Paul said, nonchalantly looking around the river. "A map," I thought to myself.

The truth was, there were no salmon running this far up in the river system—a large dam further down river prevented the fish from getting up here. And, in these waters, like most others around the province, salmon run in the fall, not the spring.

The problem was not where the lads were fishing, it was where they were *not* fishing. The best holding water was about a hundred yards down-stream, but if we wandered down to fish it, Paul and I would let the cat out of the bag. Plus, there were only two places within 300 yards of where we were standing where it was safe to cross the river. The pool we wanted to get to had to be fished from the far bank. Again, we had to either leave or wait it out until these guys left.

"Some of the lads in the club thought we'd try here. The place we usually go to on opening day is packed. About three years ago, somebody wrote it up in a fishing magazine and it's gotten worse every year."

"Yeah," I said, "funny how that works." But my irony was lost.

"You guys tried anyplace else around here?" This was the million-dollar question, and it rolled off Paul's tongue like the answer was the furthest thing from his mind. I held my breath, hoping the answer would be no. Thankfully, it was. It turned out that Soggy had tried to cross the river—in the shallow but deceivingly fast-flowing riffles—above the pool they were fishing; he "lost it," and as he drifted *through* the middle of the pool—one would assume he was too preoccupied with self-preservation to worry about getting a line in—the boys managed to haul him out. The question then becomes, "Why would you continue to fish the pool?" All the fish are hugging the bottom, saying to each other, "Hey I see the new neoprenes are in. Looks like those clear fly lines are catching on. I remember when I was a parr, we'd see hundreds of them things floating down the river. They was so thick, they'd block out the sun—yeah right, Granda—and nice hat, buddy."

It was not looking good. Crisp Christmas jackets, brand-spanking new fishing vests—one with the price tag hanging out the back—and hats, did we have hats: most of them uncrumpled, sporting nice clean bands of wool, upon which no flies were drying. Even the cork on many of the rod handles looked like it was still pristine. Several of the boys had handmade wooden landing nets dangling from the backs of their vests. Pointing at one, Paul whispered, "Nice touch. He's a trailer."

"Absolutely! No doubt about that," I agreed.

Trailers are fishermen who never step off the beaten path when accessing a river or stream. When the trail ends, so do their fishing possibilities. Trailers would never put a bag of popcorn in the microwave the wrong way up, just to see what happens. The net is usually a dead giveaway. When busting through thick cover, to access an *almost* inaccessible fishing spot, the net becomes more of a liability than an asset. I looked at Paul saying, "Tribal identification."

It was obvious, even to the untrained observer, that these guys had settled in for the day, and equally as obvious that Paul and I were going to have to leave. Then Soggy reappeared at the end of the trail and announced to the world, "Hey guys, I lost the keys!"

Suddenly, Paul and I had the river to ourselves. We picked our way across to the far bank and were drifting through the pool, looking for a rainbow or two. The morning came without warning, the sun drove away the snow, and by ten o'clock we had successfully landed several large white suckers. On a 5-weight, these fish are a blast. On my "pig" rod, they hardly put a bend in the tip. Paul had been drifting size-6 Blue Thunders, and I had gone with Torpedoes, the beadhead and fluorescent colors an ideal combination for tempting fish in cloudy water. Time—and the number of flies in our boxes, three or four drifts and then a bust-off—was quickly running out. By noon the fish would be off the feed. Judging by our acute lack of success, a case could be made that they had, in fact, never been on the feed in the first place.

For a wee bit of variety, we switched rods. Paul has a weak back, so after about a half an hour we were getting ready to switch again, when my line tightened up and I felt a head shake. Setting the hook, a 10-pound rainbow cleared the water and headed for a brush pile, topped with a nice set of overhanging willow branches. There was little in the way of a backbone in Paul's rod, and little I could do to control the fish. It cleared the water by about 3 feet, flew into the lower branches of the willows and disappeared. With the fishless fly line hanging like a limp telephone wire, drooping under a summer haze, I looked at Paul, waiting for a comment. "Strange," was all he said, then added,

"Wonder if it's nesting?" I tried to wiggle the line free from the branches. I'd never been treed by a steelhead before.

One of my most memorable treeings occurred on a still August evening, fishing with Kate for smallmouth. Just before she arrived, two massive, very cold rain storms had rolled through the area and turned off the bass. We should have been into well over fifty fish, but other than a bunch of rock bass, and an incidental catch of a 12-pound pike, things were slow.

Wandering downriver we came across two carp, backs exposed, rooting in the shallows, vacuuming up insects from the riverbed. They were medium-sized fish, around 15 pounds each. Kate was throwing a black Spike at one, and I, a size-6 Mugwump at the other. In the clear, shallow water, it was easy to see the fish inhale the Mugwump. I lifted into the fish and it tore into a solid bank of flooded bushes, settling about 10 feet back into the shrubbery, throwing the fly.

As the fish swam back into the pod, I could see the artistic-merit scorecards getting held up from its buddies: "Five. Six. Five. Six-point-five. Six." Of course, no medals would be given out until the fish passed a dope test, one the angler had obviously just failed.

I was still trying to free my fly line when Paul broke the silence. "Hey, remember that smallmouth I got?" I cut him off. "Yeah!" I drifted back to the darting dragonfly days of a warm July smallmouth trip.

On the far bank of a knee-deep river, a large bass was chasing minnows in the shallows. Shower after shower of fleeing minnows cleared the water ahead of the pursuing bulge. An easy fish to catch. Throw the fly in front of it, strip it, and in a frenzied feeding mood, instinct kicks in and the fish will hammer the fly. Easy enough to do. However, there was only about a foot of space between the trailing lower edges of the willow branches and the water surface. We could not get any closer, as the mud trail would tip the fish off to our presence.

Paul threw in a long cast, the wind caught it and the Big Joe's Crayfish skipped several times across the surface. The wind caught it again, and on the last skip it was lofted into the lower branches, leaving it dangling a good 3 feet off the water. I stared at Paul, giving him a "Way to go there, sport" look. He tightened up his line and twitched the rod tip, trying to free the fly. There was an explosion; the smallmouth cleared the water and demolished the fly. The weight of the fish ripped the line free from the branches. In silence Paul played it out and then released the 3-pound fish back into the water. I was too stunned to say much, but finally blurted out, "Well, ain't ya gonna say something?" He looked up from resharpening his hook, saying, "I was kinda wondering how I was gonna get the fly back. It's the last one I've got."

I pulled the line free, checked the fly and switched rods with Paul. He motioned upriver. "There's a few trailers setting up at that top pool. I guess we're done."

"Yeah. Let's cut in here, scoot down the bank, cross over and come back up their side." We did.

It turned out that four fishermen—two float and two fly—were just starting to fish the pool when we got back up to them. "Gettin' any?" I asked.

"Nah, we just got here. How about you?"

"Yeah," I said, "We hooked a big salmon in here, and it took us *way* downriver. Hell of a fish." Paul jumped in, "Only one we had on. Spooled him twice. We've been here all night, haven't seen a rainbow." One of the fly fishermen, sporting a brand-new vest, looked at our fly gear and asked, "What did you get him on: an Emerger, Streamer or Nymph?" Well now, feeling obliged to pick one out of the three, I went with "An Emerger. Something small and black. Last one I had in my box. Too bad he busted me off."

"Yeah, too bad. I'd liked to have seen it."

I'm thinking, "I bet you would." I looked at his rod, asking, "Is that a brand-new rod?"

"Yeah, I got it for Christmas. First chance I've had to use it."

"You might want to try scuffing up the handle. Kind of like Sir Clifford Curzon." He looked at me like I'd lost it.

"Curzon, the great pianist, died in the 'eighties, used to take a chunk of sandpaper and lightly go over the tops of the piano keys so that his fingers wouldn't slip when they got all sweaty. Do the same with that new cork; it helps you hang onto the pole."

As we started to head up the trail, Paul added, "We got this spot off the Internet. It's not all it's cracked up to be."

I added, "Only good thing was the map."

Willie and the Pike

Too young for a full day of school, and too keen to keep from fishing, Willie set off on his daily trip for early May crappies. Crunching on the dry, gray roadside gravel, his "lucky" fire-engine-red gum boots strode with purpose. As each step became slightly quicker and more determined than the last, it wasn't hard to tell that the boots, and everything attached to them, were on a mission. It's tough to hold a good man down, especially when he's got his own custom-built 4-foot rod and a fly box. Sporting a Magic Marker drawing of a cased caddis, this was no ordinary fly box. This was *his* box. A green plastic fly box, personalized with colorful scribbles of crayon and a much-faded Peter Rabbit sticker. Inside, stuck in the white Styrofoam, were the flies he had learned to count to ten with. Row upon row of cast-off patterns from my tying bench, and those he'd

scooped from my boxes. His routine for rustling up some flies was always the same. It was a deliciously simple game of "I believe," and we both knew the outcome before it started. Opening up one of my boxes, he'd pick up a fly and say:

"E-on?"

"Yeah."

"Iz'at a Booby?" (He knew it wasn't.)

"No, I bee-leeve it is a Winkie, old chap."

"Hmmmmm. A Winkie. Hmmmmm ... Iz'at a good fly?" (He knew it was.)

"I bee-leeve it is, Willie. It will catch pike, perch, bass, trout and salmon."

"Hmmmmm. Well E-on, I bee-leeve I don't have one."

"Hmmmmm."

"We-llllllllll, I bee-leeve ther'z a wittle space in my box."

"Hmmmmm. I bee-leeve you'd better stick him in the foam."

"Thanks, I bee-leeve I will." Forcing the fly into his box, he'd look at it and say,

"It's boo-ti-ful."

With the chubby fingers of his left hand clutching the box, and his flyrod riding like a rifle over his right shoulder, Willie worked at scuffing up a larger dust trail as he headed toward the pond. In the contrail, two steps behind him but well within arm's reach, I carried the snacks, the juice, the equipment bag, the camera and, just in case, a large bath towel. The lake was glass. Behind the trees at the far side of the lake, the sun was slowly slipping toward the horizon. A week from now, the mosquitoes would make fishing at this time of day very painful. Near a bank of bulrushes, a few geese bobbed up and down, sending feeding ripples crawling across the still, smooth water. The pond was duckless. For several minutes we stood in silence at the edge of the road, watching the lazy scene unfold.

"It'z gonna be a good day for crappies." It was almost sunset, but he was close.

"Sure is, Willie. What ya gonna use?"

"Weeelllll, hmmmm, maybe a Crunchy Caddis." He opened his box and scanned the flies. "A-ha!"

"What ya got, Willie?"

"Weeelllll, maybe a Cat's Whisker or a Booby." For obvious reasons the Booby was a hit, and the first time his grandmother heard him utter the name, the fly became a catalyst for an interesting and very heated conversation. However, had he said Bitch Creek Nymph, it could have been much worse.

"A Cat's Whisker will work."

"Okay, okay, I know," was the excited reply.

"What?"

"A Fuzzy Wuzzy."

"Big or little?"

"Hmmm, wittle. Crappies likes wittle stuff." He glanced over the flies once more, changed his mind, handed me a Cat's Whisker, closed the box and headed down the twisty trail toward a concrete slab hidden among the sprouting bulrushes at the edge of the pond.

There are no crappies in Scotland (although the point could be argued if an English soccer team is visiting). One of my first forays into the angling world was with my da for spring pike, to a pond near the town of Hamilton. We went with a pound of bacon, eggs, kippers, sausages, a loaf of bread, a frying pan, a pot to make tea, a jug of water and fishing gear. As the first few rays of sunlight danced in the morning dew, he led me through a "shortcut" over a 10-foot-high, knee-skinning wall, trespassing across a horse-racing track and a golf course. "Son, tae get tae the pond," my father informed me, "we just have tae nip across a fairway or two, so keep a keen eye oot fir balls." Never once was there any mention of the dangers from the sound of "thundering hoofs" or the ramifications of the term "Private."

Every trip with my da was an adventure, and just for fun he'd always play up any dangers, real or imaginary, and likewise any risks. It might be bears, wasp nests, the police, adders, quicksand or the ever-popular recital of Robert Burns's poem "Tam O' Shanter"—a tale about a tipsy Scot coming across a midnight dance of witches, the dead and the devil. Tam evades capture when his horse crosses the keystone of a bridge. Everybody knows that evil spirits and such, just can't cross a keystone and you should never "step on the cracks." From memory, my da could recite most of Burns's poems, but with this one he deliberately mixed up the lines to achieve the effect he desired, usually when we were watching bats deep in the woods.

"Or, catch'd wi' warlocks in the mirk / By Alloway's auld haunted kirk ... / Coffins stood round, like open presses, / That shaw'd the Dead in their last dresses." Then he'd add, "Remember, son, if I canna see yi, I canna help yi."

We didn't catch much, but among the sprouting bulrushes a slightly smoky bacon sandwich, peppered with a dusting of cinders and ash, has never tasted better.

I watched the back of Willie's red TVOntario T-shirt disappearing between the bulrushes. This shirt was payment for a gig he did on the show "Studio 2" with "Lucky," his brother Ben's goldfish—won as a prize at the ping-pong-ball toss at a local fair. Like the boots, this shirt was "lucky" and proudly worn on every fishing trip.

"Hey, Willie. Did you hear that? I think it was a Woozle!" Willie froze and, thanking God for Winnie the Pooh, I caught up to him. *Ssshhh! Don't move.* With eyes like saucers, he was hardly breathing. Seconds seemed like an eternity. Then I said, "Aw, it was just a goose, Willie, just a goose."

He turned. We looked at each other and, in unison, said, "Silly. Old. Goose!"

Being unable to see over or through the vegetation, he still looked a wee bit uneasy. Pointing skyward, I hollered, "To the Bat Cave!" He turned and started splashing through the ankle-deep water and mud. Ten minutes later—it would have been sooner had we not discovered, and fully investigated, a painted turtle enjoying the last of the sunlight and the radiant heat from a large rock—we arrived. The concrete slab we'd fish from was slightly submerged, inches beneath the high-water level of the spring.

"Gimmie the rule, Willie!"

"If you can't see me ... You can't save me."

"You got it my fine, young fishing friend, *and* you"—I playfuly poked him in the tummy—"win a cone on the way home."

I put the gear down on a large log and tied 8 feet of monolfilament onto his fly line. Half-singing, I said, "On goes the fly, du-du-doo!" He answered with "On goes the glasses, du-du-doo!" From the "secret pocket" sewn by his mum into the inside of his *Lion King* track pants, he pulled out a pair of sunglasses and put them on. By now I'd tied the Cat's Whisker he'd given me onto the leader. His first roll cast sent the fly out 20 feet. It disappeared. He counted it down. "One-tug-tug. Two-tug-tug. Three-tug ... E-on, is four after three?"

"Yip, four is after three, then five is next."

"Four-tug-tug ... FISH! I got a crappie! In you come, wittle guy."

He stripped in a few feet of line, held up the rod and pushed the tip behind him into the air, swinging the fish toward him. Reaching in, I cradled the 6-inch fish in the water. Again, from the secret pocket, he produced a set of needlenose pliers, then carefully removed the barbless hook. He said, "See ya!" And I slipped my hand away from the fish, releasing it.

"He was boo-ti-ful!"

"Sure was. Silver and green with black spots and a white tummy. Are ya gonna get another?"

"Yip. I like the 'ellow eyes." He rolled the fly back out onto the water, and I set about putting together my flyrod. I was looking for pike. He caught and set free three more fish by the time I was ready to go. On outings with our club, Willie had been the center of attention by showing "the lads" how easily he could unhook the fish he caught. This was his badge of honor. He was as skilled at catching crappies as he and Ben—owner of Lucky—were at playing with Lego. In one afternoon he caught and released fifty fish. Quite the accomplishment for a lad who could not as yet count past ten.

Two weeks before this trip, we were fishing in the same spot. He'd selected a fluorescent Red Wiggler fly "just 'coz it looks right" and was hooking a fish on almost every cast. We started around midafternoon, and, by supper time, with very little help, he had caught and released fifty crappies. Equally as important, he never changed the pattern he started with, learning that, when something is working, stick with it, rather than trying to find another fly that might be more productive. Just about every fly-fishing guide and instructor I know would be over the moon if other fly fishermen were to pick up on that tip. The fluorescent Red Wiggler is a fine winter steelhead pattern, and until then I'd never thought to use it for crappies, although my clients and I have done so many times since.

In the car on the way home, Willie looked over and said, "E-on, how many fish did I get again?"

"Fifty, Willie. You got fifty crappies."

"Iz'at a lot?"

"Yip. It sure is. Most folk don't get that many."

He had a small frown as he turned to look out of the window. After several miles and three rounds of Stan Rogers' "Xerox Line," closely followed by two verses of the spooky version of "The Teddy Bears' Picnic," he started up the conversation with: "E-on?"

"What's up, my little fly-fishing buddy?"

"How many did you get?"

"I don't know. I wasn't counting." (It was easy to see where *this* was going.)

"Did you get fifty?"

"No, not really."

"So ... hmmmmm ... I got more than you?"

"A-ha?"

"Wow, 'n' I'm not even a pro-fesh-on-al."

The following morning, at nine o'clock, when the local sports store opened its doors, I was the first one through them, buying a trophy to commemorate his achievement.

Although this was one of Willie's trips for spring crappies, the pike season had just opened. He would be as happy as a clam, hauling in and releasing the "wittle guys" all day long, but I fancied something a bit bigger. Knowing that post-spawn pike are aggressive, I tied on a large red and white Dexter, size 2, and cast it out toward a very "pikeable"-looking spot.

"E-on, how come you're wearing waders?"

"Well, if you fall in, or if a fish gets tangled up in the stumps, I can do a rescue."

"Hmmmm."

Soon he was into his twelfth or thirteenth fish and I was yet to get a hit. Most of the time I was watching him, rather than paying attention to what I was doing. "Jeezus, he's good. I can see him ending up with his own fishing show one day."

With a wave and "There you go wittle guy. Bye-bye," another crappie swam away.

I threw out a long cast. As soon as the fly had dropped down through the water, disappearing from sight, I started my slow-slow-quick-quick-slow retrieve. A deadly dance for coldwater pike, and the outer limit of my rhythmical abilities. When the fly was 20 feet out from the tip of the rod, there was a flash of white and I instinctively lifted into the fish. With coldwater pike, it is best to gently lift into the fish when you see the big white flash, rather than waiting for the tug. Even though the pike is a fierce predator and a toothy game fish with a mean set of canines, the key word is "gently." A hard, fast hook set will pull the fly away from the fish and well clear of its mouth. A 15-pound Great Northern, a Devil Fish, or good old *Mr. Esox lucius,* as those with "the Latin" would say, cleared the water. With no sign of the fly dangling from the pike, I knew it was well hooked, most probably in the roof of the mouth, about halfway back. As the line started to dance across the water, I switched rods with Willie. "Ho, man! It's a biggie! It's a biggie!" Hearing the commotion, the geese took off across the lake like a pack of guys wearing fur coats at a "Save the Seals" convention.

The handle on the reel was a spinning blur as the fish ripped out line.

"Keep the rod tip up, don't touch the reel, and bow to him when he jumps. When he wants to run, just let him go. Remember? Just let him go—he'll come back again."

"HO, MAN!"

I'm not sure if he heard me or if it was the results of our practicing on the driveway during the winter. But the rod tip was definitely "up" and there was a noticeable absence of color in his chubby, round cheeks—and mine.

"HO, MAN!"

The fish jumped, and the rod tip dropped.

"HO, MAN!"

"If he comes toward us, strip in line and dump it. I'll take care of it for you."

"HO, MAN!"

For the next fifteen minutes I said nothing, letting him enjoy what was going on, and letting him figure things out for himself. If the fish got off, someday there would be another. Best that I should shut up and concentrate on keeping his line free from tangles. By the time he'd brought the pike in close enough for me to perform a "G and L" (grab and lift), his face was as red as his gum boots, his knuckles looked like piano keys, and he was shaking from the adrenaline rush.

He was bubbling over with Christmas-morning excitement when I pulled the fish clear of the water and he saw it.

"HO! MAN! HO! MAN! HO! MAN!"

At about 3 feet long, from his and just about anyone else's point of view, the fish was a giant, a monster of mammoth proportions. He reached into his track pants pocket for the needlenose pliers. With the pike giving him the "Go ahead. I dare you" look, I thought to myself: "Ho! Man!"

On the one hand, and in a spot where I'd like to keep them, were his small, soft, inexperienced fingers. On the other, and a disaster in the making, a highly aggressive predator with a mouthful of razor-sharp teeth. From the tip of its snout to behind its eyes, the pike's head was at least three times longer than Willie's hand. Not sure what to do next, and in an effort to free up a wee bit of "don't panic" time, I decided to cradle the fish in the water. With a keen naivety he clutched the pliers, blissfully unaware of the danger in what he was contemplating. He didn't know it, but this was as close as he was going to get to the fish—or more importantly, the fly.

"I got him on, so I let him go. That's the rules. Right, E-on?" The thoroughness of my teachings had just sneaked up and bit me in the ass. "That's the rules, Willie."

Deeply concerned and stuck with a "phalangeal predacious predicament," I had to come up with something, but I didn't want to back down on any of the sage bits of wisdom I had imparted to him over the years. The typical guy stuff like: If you get a fish on, you let it go. Don't kill a fish or an animal unless you're going to gut it, cook it and wash the dishes when you're finished. Never pee into the wind. When you're writing your name in the snow, dot your i's as you make them. Better to run out and not finish your name rather than risking the taunts of your snow-peeing peers for sloppy "pen"-manship.

"Willie, this is the first pike you've landed all by yourself. I bee-leeve I'd like to show you the best way to get the fly back, just so you don't hurt the fish."

He pondered my request.

"Weeeell, I bee-leeve dats okay."

Prying the pliers from his fingers (the little bugger wasn't going down without a fight), I knelt down and leaned toward the fish. The flaw in the plan was that, having been in the cold, oxygenated water, El Fish-o was now much revived-o, so things might not go as smoothly as I first thought. Willie had crouched down to take a good close look at the unhooking. It all happened too quickly.

Half lifting the fish with my right hand, I got the pliers near its mouth, but it squirmed, sending up a shower of water. Its mouth opened, showing a full set of teeth. Receiving a close-up view, which was just a wee bit too close, Willie toppled backwards. To steady himself, he grabbed at my left arm, the one with the pliers, pushing it forward and sliding my hand into the gaping maw. Conveniently, the pike closed its jaws around my hand, firmly wedging it in its mouth. Blood—my blood—began to spill over its lower jaw and drip onto the water, spreading out like a fine layer of bath oil in a warm tub. All I could think was, "Uh, oh!"

Willie stood up, steadied himself against my shoulder and peered at the fish. Then, as kids often do, he stated the obvious: "You're bleeding."

Not sure of my closing number or what I would do for an encore, I calmly said, "A wee bit, Willie, just a wee bit."

"Does it hurt?"

A pillar of stability, I faked unconcern. "Nah! Any other questions?" I had a feeling that, had my hand not been numbed from holding the fish in the brisk and chilly water, I would have been feeling a lot more pain.

"How come ... how come, if you're bleeding, it don't hurt?"

With a few more pressing issues to deal with, I passed on answering. But, having not received one, the kid pressed on.

"E-on, pike is vewy danger-wus."

"What?"

"Pike. Pike is vewy danger-wus."

"I guess they are." Gently pulling on the needlenose end, through the far side of the mouth, I retrieved the pliers. Then—and, God help me, someone should have slapped me silly for this one—I tried to make a fist inside the pike's mouth, hoping the action might somehow pry its jaws apart. All I succeeded in doing was rolling my hand around, producing more lacerations. Willie was looking quite anxious about the whole affair. "Best to get him involved," I thought to myself. As for the pike, had it not been working on masticating and predigesting my hand, I'm sure it would have been grinning. No doubt it was thinking, "If I get this down, I won't have to eat again all year. And hey! This tastes like chicken."

"Hey, Willie. Wet your hands and grab the pike, just behind his gills. Don't put your fingers near them or you'll get stuck too!" Quick to help, hands and arms were instantly immersed and soaked up to the elbows, then latched around the fish.

I worked the pliers into the front of the jaw and forced the handles apart. It gave me just enough space to slip my hand out. The fish wriggled, but the kid held on. Having sustained multiple lacerations, I decided to lip-land the pike. Why not? A few more razor-like slashes or punctures from the flesh-piercing canines wouldn't be that bad. Gripping the front of the lower jaw between my thumb and first finger, I reached in with the pliers and grabbed the fly, asking Willie if he could hold the pliers to help pull the fly out. His eyes lit up. Without hesitation he reached for the bright blue plastic handles. As soon as he had

control of the pliers, I let go. Just in case it all went wrong, I quickly closed my hand—my only *good* hand—over his. The debarbed fly fell out as soon as we touched it, but together we *pulled* the hook free.

"A-ha! Victory!" he said triumphantly. Beaming, he held up the bloodied and slimy fly.

"Great job there, Doctor Will. Say bye-bye, Mr. Pikie."

"Bye-bye, wittle guy."

I dipped the fish into the water and let go of the lower jaw. The fish did not, however, slip off into the depths. Instead, it sat inches below the surface, staring up at its captors. This shocked Willie more than the carnage he had witnessed over the past ten minutes. He looked at me, raised his eyebrows and, with a slight tremble in his voice, said, "Uh, oh!" Thinking, "We're not going through this again," I poked the fish with my rod tip.

Sulking, it swam away.

"E-on?"

"Yes, Doctor Will."

"You're bleedin'."

"Yep."

"Wanna go get a sticky plaster?"

"Yep, great idea." He looked at me, pointed to the trail in the bulrushes and—though I know not why—announced "Victory!"

I headed for home with a half a roll of toilet-paper bandage wrapped around my hand, administered in the front seat of the car by Doctor Will. If you're asking why was there a roll of toilet paper in the car, you have obviously never taken any long trips with a pack of kids. Sighing with relief, I pulled into the driveway. Willie unclipped his seatbelt and was polishing off the last of a red licorice stick he had traded for the cone I'd promised him earlier in the day.

The "bandage" had been dumped in the garbage can outside the store. It is bad enough to go home knowing there will be little sympathy and many taunts, but showing up with half a roll of blood-stained toilet paper wrapped around your hand is just asking for it.

Willie grabbed his boots from the floor, pulled off his wet, muddied socks and stuffed them into the boots. On our trip out, his shortcut—a trail he *assured* me he'd been down hundreds of times—held water a wee bit deeper than he'd suspected. He got stuck 10 feet short of the safety of the roadside and *terra firma*. I knew he would before we started, but he had to learn the old stay-on-the-beaten-path thing. Sinking up to his knees in the quagmire, he stepped out of his boots. Under his caution of "Don't get blood on my TVO shirt," I had to do a rescue. I plucked him out, tucked him under my arm with the flyrods, waded out and set him down with the gear on the gravel. I went back in for the boots, while, from the safety of dry land, he directed maneuvers and guarded our stuff against sneak attacks from raccoons, muskrats or beavers.

He sniffed at his boots, looked across the seat and said, "Oh man, these stink and they're kinda squishy!" I could have told him why but went with "A-ha."

As we neared home, he said, "E-on, you're lucky pikes iz not ven-i-must."

"Ven-i-must?"

"Ven-i-must, like a king cobra, 'coz you'd be dead."

I switched off the engine, but before it had time to die he was out of the car, clutching his boots. With his bare feet slapping on the concrete, he headed at full speed down the path toward the side door of the house. The boots never quite made it to the door. Without slowing down, he scored a direct hit by pitching them across the lawn, bouncing them off the coiled-up garden hose. Sitting behind the steering wheel, thinking, "Perfect practice makes perfect," I heard his big announcement of "E-on got bit by a pike," closely followed by, "My boots iz kinda squishy, but dats OKAY!"

I washed off the wounds in my hand with peroxide and soaked it in hot salt water. The following day it was swollen and it was difficult to bend my knuckles. Days later, things returned to normal, but, by then, Willie had told everyone he met about how "danger-wus" pike were and how he'd saved me. No one, from the cashiers at the grocery store, to the members of the Casual Dress Fly Fishing Club and tackle-shop owners, was spared. The lads in the club and in the tackle shops encouraged him to replay the incident every time they met him. "Tell us again, Willie, how danger-wus pike are and how you saved E-on." He did. And often.

Two weeks later I arranged to meet some fellow fly fishermen for an evening of crappie fishing at the concrete pad. Through the early afternoon, Willie and I were out collecting fiddleheads and looking for spring peeper frogs. The fiddleheads were easy to find; the frogs much harder, although he did get two. Plucking the green ostrich-fern (*Matteuccia struthiopteris*) sprouts from the damp, dank ground, we were on a roll. They are easy to collect and we were going through the "just take what you need but leave lots to make more" routine. They are delicious and we loved eating them—boiled in salt water, served steaming hot and smothered in butter—as much as we did collecting them.

A word of warning: Although fiddleheads are easy to find, be careful. Bracken fern (*Pteridium aquilinum*), the type of plant you might find in the base of a corsage, looks similar to ostrich fern but is carcinogenic. Luckily, ostrich ferns prefer moist, shady areas, rich in humus and all that wonderfully earthy, musky and smelly type of stuff like rotting leaves. Bracken ferns, however, tend to grow in dry areas and in poorer soil like that found in roadside ditches. Generally, there are three heads on a single, smooth, bare bracken-fern stalk, and brackens are smaller and darker than ostrich ferns, which have one large head on the end of a hairy stem. Unless you are absolutely sure what you are collecting (and, if friends are helping you, you harbor no misgivings about their intentions), pick up fiddleheads at the grocery store rather than in the great outdoors. Sure, you will miss out on the thrill of the hunt and the excitement of going through hours of careful stalking when pursuing the wild fiddlehead. Yet passing on these simple country pleasures is a small price to pay for a healthy liver—plus you won't have to carve a batch of decoys to lure them in. As for the intentions of your friends, be careful: they might have an eye on your fishing gear, should you mysteriously "pull up your peg" and head skyward into the light.

By the time we finished having way too much fun collecting the fiddleheads, thus arriving late at the concrete pad, my buddies were already set up. We exchanged the usual "How's it going? Any bites?" Willie pulled me aside and, with a shout, "whispered" into my ear: "E-on! Those guys have my spot!" Seeing the opportunity for a lesson in compromise, understanding and respect for the needs of the angling brotherhood, I went with "Well, Willie, it's not your spot and they were here first, so you will just have to find a place where you can cast. Don't be shy—ask. It's not their spot and it's not your spot. I'll save you if they wanna get tough. Right?" "Right!" he said, furrowing his brows, and putting on his best brave and determined face. I tied a Cat's Whisker onto his leader, nodding to the guys and motioning for them to give the lad a bit of space. By the time they had, Willie had weasled himself into front and center, announcing, "Hey! Hey, you guys. Gimmie some space. I'm with the Big Guy!" Then, without missing a heartbeat, he added, "You gett'n any?" They shuffled around, giving me a few subtle thumbs-up signals and stifled laughter, then severally replied, "Not much." I made a mental note to try that one again.

Very little in the way of fishy frolics was happening, and the mosquitoes were starting to make their presence felt. The lads were digging through pockets and grumbling about the acute lack of fish. The eternal optimist, Willie continued roll-casting out his Cat's Whisker, counting it down and tugging it back in. Even he, the man of fifty fish, was having a hard time getting a tap. The resident osprey had been doing a lot of circling and had made many dives but it, too, was coming up short. Things were definitely starting to wind down. Willie had given the lads a graphic description of where I'd been attacked by the pike and informed them that pike were "vewy danger-wus," and would eat baby ducks, frogs and "mush-rats."

The largest pike we had caught, until Willie's fish showed up, was about 6 pounds and hardly the type of beastie capable of bringing down a baby mallard. If we were taking 6- and 7-pounders, who spawned them and how big were they now? Applying the same streamside slide rule, Willie's pike was around the 15-pound mark and about seven or eight years old, so whoever spawned that fish must, by any standard, be huge. Do the math—so we did. Science has shown that female pike grow larger than the males do, and they live longer, so we worked on the stats for the female. Most female pike will start to reproduce when they are three or four years old and about 5 or 6 pounds. Assuming that the female who dropped the eggs and spawned Willie's fish was still alive, add about seven years to its life and you have a fish of about twelve years of age. A pike that age could conceivably weigh in at more than 25 pounds, and be pushing 30. This was all idle chitchat and donut-shop speculation, but it was a frightening prospect and a good excuse to buy a bigger flyrod. Was it a tackle-shop daydream or just another big-fish fantasy? Willie's fish, we assumed, must have been the one we had watched over the years taking down baby ducks, but perhaps its mother was responsible for the disappearing goslings and the many witnessed duckling demises.

We've all seen the cute bundles of "fluffy duck down" about the size of a yellow tennis ball, accessorized with bright red feet and a brown beak. At Wimbledon there would be a flurry of activity should those two items ever happen to get mixed up. "Puškauskas, the Lithuanian tennis ace, is serving for match point." Splat! "Ooooh! They are going to have to check the rulebook for a decision on that one."

But, there they go, bobbing in a small armada behind their parents, motoring along, with their little legs just a-pumping, making with those cricket-like *cheep-cheep-cheeps*. Perhaps they are striking out for a glorious patch of weed, or perhaps they are just enjoying the feeling of being alive, out of the egg, with the wind gently stroking their young feathers and filling their nostrils with the joys of nature. Full of hope, they paddle along, humming a few bars of "There once was an ugly duckling," with an innocence as yet untarnished by the cruel realization that they are, in fact, ducks and will never be swans. Listening to the frogs and the redwinged blackbirds, I wonder, does it get any better than this? Close your eyes. Look. LOOK! I know you can see them smiling, then, then they are gone. Sipped leisurely from below the surface the way a trout would take down a mayfly. As the story goes, "The mother duck said *quack, quack, quack* and only two came swimming back."

"Hey! Willie! Time to go, Snert. The bugs'll be getting bad soon."

"Aw, E-on. Just one more cast."

Someone bowed. "Haaa! I see the boy has learned well, Mast'ha James." One more cast is the key to all good fishing trips but, in angling households, the cause of many nights on the sofa. I had no choice. "Okay. On you go. You might get something."

We were aimlessly looking out at the osprey taking one last shot at a fish, and small amounts of money were riding on the bird's performance. It hovered, dropped into a dive, said, "Screw it!" and pulled up short of the water. It ambled off toward the setting sun, with deliberate and dejected wingbeats. As the cash changed hands, someone whispered, "Christ, even it's not catching anything. Poor Willie, his confidence will be shattered. We've been here about four hours and we haven't had a tap. Must be a low barometric pressure or something." A voice added, "What do you know about barometric pressure? You've only started watching the TV forecasts since they started putting babes in front of those maps. You don't give 'a monkey's' about the swirly-cloudy-thingies, receding high-pressure ridges or falling pressure. All you want to see are receding hemlines and falling necklines."

I threw in, "Does your wife know you think like that?" and someone added, "Nah! He's been fooling her over the twenty years they've been married by actively *not* thinking. At least, that's what she keeps telling me." We all saw the white flash at Willie's fly. And the silence was immediate.

When he felt the tug and set the hook, Willie's rod bent double.

"Got one!"

A pike cleared the water. Actually it vaulted out of the water, tail-walked for several feet, then dropped back in with a spectacular splash. It was well over 25 pounds. It was Willie's panicked voice that broke the collectively stunned silence.

"I got a g'aligator! I Got A G'aligator! I GOT A G'ALIGATOR!!!"

"Keep the rod tip up, just like the last time, Willie." I motioned to the boys to keep their mouths firmly shut. From the get-go, Willie hadn't a dog's chance of landing the fish. On a full-size rod with lots of backing, he might have had a slim one, but with his 4-foot rod, small reel and 12 yards of backing, he didn't have a snowball's.

With its mouth wide open, exposing both the white interior and its canine teeth, it jumped again, shaking its head and flaring its gill covers. There was a collective "Jeez-uss," from the mesmerized crowd.

"Hold me, E-on! I'm go'n in, E-ON!! EEEEE–ONNNNN!!!"

"Oh yeah, the kid. Yeah right, now I remember." I grabbed his shoulders and said, "Got ya." The fish was almost pulling the rod from his hands. He was leaning backward into my waders and holding on for dear life. His pole was bent to the handle and I was waiting for the *SNAP!*—the all-too-familiar sound a rod makes when it packs it in, surrendering to a fish that is just too big. Willie came to the end of his backing. Thirty-seven yards out, the line tightened up, the fish boiled at the surface and the fly pulled free. Reeling in and flipping the fly back out, "Oh you ... you ... waskil, I'll get ya!" was all he said.

As we tried to come to grips with the evening's proceedings, there was much head scratching, baseball-cap adjusting and eyebrow raising. Willie kept on casting. The best comment was: "Low barometric pressure, my ass. THAT was the reason we weren't getting any crappies. Even the 6-inchers would be a mere morsel!" Our excitement carried over and infected Willie. He was spooked and fascinated by the size of the fish, so we described it as being about the same size as he was.

The following day, Willie and I were in an art-supply store, in the heart of downtown Guelph, buying pencils. Otto, the owner, who knew Willie very well since we were in there two or three times a week, came in from the storeroom and shouted down the length of the shop: "Hey, Willie, getting any fish?"

"Well, actually, I got a pike as big as me." "Well," "actually" and "I hope you know" were his current catch phrases. Things like "I hope you know that bears eat fruit" and "Well, actually, E-on, I'd like a cookie."

I gave Otto "the nod," verifying that what he was about to hear was in fact true. "Is that so? You better tell me about it?" On cue, Willie gave him the full account of his tussle with the fish, and its size. The classic saga of man and fish lasted for about fifteen minutes, approximately twelve minutes longer than he actually had the fish on the line. Willie was going on about how big the fish was, how mean it looked and "how danger-wus pike iz." An elderly lady who had missed the part about what fly he had been using listened to the end of his blow-by-blow recital. This sweet, grandmotherly woman in her early seventies looked down at Willie, who was out of breath and had worked up quite a sweat, and said, "What did you get him on, little boy? A worm?" He drew in a deep breath, puffed up his chest and, with Herculean pride, said, "No, m'am! I fly fish!"

Over the years we have fished the concrete pad many times and no one else has hooked into a pike larger than 8 pounds. Like most unsolved mysteries, there is little in the way of an explanation for why Willie took both big fish or why a pike of 25 pounds or so, quite capable of bringing down "baby mush-rats," would grab at a fly half the size of a computer shift-key. It is all quite remarkable, but—and it's a very big but—it's always difficult to classify the unexplained.

"And the mother duck said ..."

Embrace the Wind

Today, as usual on any summer morning, around five-thirty the cardinal outside my bedroom window went nuts. I lay in bed, listening to him singing his little heart out, imagining his head bobbing up and down with each note of the *Weet-weet-weet-weet-weet-weet*. It is hard not to like this bird, with its scarlet plumage, spiky head crest and black mask around its thick stubby beak giving it a jesterial and mischievous look. Cardinals are very affectionate, often feeding their mates seeds from the bird feeder outside the kitchen window. I once said the prettiest thing I had seen was a cardinal sitting in a crimson foliage of a Japanese red maple, but I was wrong. Last spring, waiting for his turn at the bird bath, one was sitting in among the blooms of a purple lilac bush. There are no words to describe how stunning and spectacular the scarlet splash was, surrounded by the cascades of delicate purple lilac spikes.

This one, perched in the lower branches of the Chinese elm tree not 10 feet from the bedroom window, was waking up the neighborhood. And he was giving it big licks, going for broke with every note. When he decided to finish—or he had temporarily shorted-out from the singing strain—and was fully satisfied that not a living soul within two blocks was asleep, he passed the torch to the robins and the grackles. They loudly carried on, picking up the pace and pushing up the decibels. Then a few crows and some blue jays got into the act, so falling back to sleep was out of the question.

Listening to the dawn chorus, my heart was racing; the sunlight stretching through the window blinds had a heavy feel to it. I knew a storm was on the way.

On this quiet Sunday morning, the birds had scaled it down to a riot by the time I'd backed out of the driveway. In pursuit of pure pleasure, I was racing to meet the storm.

The orange needle on the speedometer flickered and hovered over the 80 mark as I pulled clear of the city limits. This was my first of the season, so I was more than eager to get on with it, but not eager enough to press *down* on the gas pedal and pick *up* a speeding ticket. As I headed northeasterly, I saw that the sky to my left was blue and clear. Behind me was a wall of battleship gray, fringed with pale blue, fading to a black center. To the south, it was the same. I was slightly ahead of the leading edge of the storm, but in the rearview mirror everything was black. The window was rolled down and I was playing "airplane" with my left hand in the slipstream flowing past the car.

The road was dry, the asphalt covered in a gray dusting of dirt. Thankfully there were no raindrops on the windshield, but I knew I had to hurry. Plants along the ditches had a gray look to them, their leaves covered in the powder thrown up from the passing cars and trucks over the last few days. Even the tall stately bull thistle, with its winged silvery stems was grayer than usual. Its crown of purple flowers was tarnished and dull from the white soot.

No rain for almost two weeks had left the air tinder-dry, but now everything reeked of humidity, and all of Nature was begging for the storm to bring instant relief.

Above the static on the car radio, the six o'clock weather report was warning, "As several storms from Michigan ... *(Skhiwwwissh)* ... roll across Southern Ontario ... *(Skhiwwwissh)* ... expect local thunderstorms, some of which might be heavy at times." This, I was hoping, was going to be one of those times. *"Yeee, haaa!!!"* I hollered out the window to a field of cows, while cursing myself for not throwing a few bluegrass cassette tapes into the car before I left. Nothing like a battalion of banjos, mandolins and wailing fiddles to get you in an upbeat, happy mood. Okay, maybe a stirring rendition of "Flower of Scotland" on the bagpipes could do the same, dispeling the rumor that the pipes are, in fact, the missing link between music and noise.

Environment Canada had not issued either a severe-weather warning or a severe-weather watch, so things were going to work out just fine. The sky was not vexed or angry or adorned with swirls of enraged black clouds. It was not a seething violent mass, to threaten life, damage property or spawn tornadoes. This sky was a solid wall of dark gray, ominous by volume, but willing to be playful.

Thirty minutes later, the tires scratched the dry stones as I pulled off the road and rolled to a stop in the gravel parking spot near the river. Several silver snails crawled down windows, and the wind was noticeable by its absence. Around the clearing, the leaves on the black walnuts were limp, and the branches of the willows were weeping more than usual. No birds were singing; there were no butterflies; and with the squirrels and chipmunks nowhere to be seen, it was obvious that Nature was about to change and those in the know were hunkering down.

Time was just about to run out.

I popped open the trunk, and as I was scrambling into my waders at the back of the car, flashes of sheet lightning danced and the sky pulsed. Heavier raindrops were landing in the dirt around my boots, each one sending up a small dusty puff before becoming a slowly widening stain. I could hear the heavy metallic thunks on the car roof. On the ground, the dark mosaic had begun to grow rapidly, creeping, joining and spreading like fingers of frost on a winter window.

I finished setting the reel into the seat of my 6-weight rod. As I was stringing the double-tapered floating line through the guides, spots of rain were cooling the back of my neck. Like they were on the ground, the stains were creeping across the fabric of my green Funky Fish T-shirt. (This may be one of the greatest quirks afforded to an artist—to have an idea, draw it, silk-screen the shirt, then wear it.) Quickly, I tied on a 10-foot, 6-pound leader and a size-2 Spike. This spun-and-clipped deer-hair pattern is arguably my number one surface fly for summer smallmouth. And, more important, it's a treat for the eyes when fishing in the rain. It looks like a wee hedgehog floating among the circles, dancing and drifting along the eddies and having a fun time in the riffles.

The drops were now beating with an increasing rhythm on the roof of the car. I could feel the air temperature slipping as each twist of the wind brought the storm closer. More drips landed on my arms and neck; the splotches grew larger on my shirt. The gusts were now closer together, each slightly stronger than the one before. The approaching dull thumps of thunder were getting louder. This was going to be awfully tight.

BOOM! and the fillings in my teeth rattled.

I propped the rod up against a large tree, grabbed my tackle bag, slammed the trunk lid down and dove to the car—no mean feat in a pair of waders— and, when the rubber I was wearing hit the vinyl of the driver's seat, I squeaked to an abrupt stop. As I closed the door, the sky opened up.

With these types of thunderstorms, the leading edge is always exciting but very brief. Down here on the ground, when the storm hits, the trees shake, large branches rattle around, twigs and small branches and leaves are torn from wooden limbs.

The rain is driven hard onto the ground. On the road surface it bounces back up, giving the illusion that the road is a river, shrouded in a 3-inch-high, soft smoky mist. You can smell the chemicals, spilled, dripped or leaked from worn car seals as they are atomized from the road surface and carried along at the edge of the wind. Soon the smell is gone, but the chemicals are not. Trapped on the water, they flow off into some roadside ditch or find a storm sewer from which they will eventually slip into the nearest stream or creek. Often there is a slight film on top of the run-off. A sparkling rainbow silently swims along, until it finds something to cling onto, coat and smother. And, for the fly-fisherman, the wind and the rain offer up some very interesting, but not insurmountable or unsolvable, casting problems.

Even during the heaviest part of the rainfall, quite often the base of a large trunk, and the underside of the lower branches, will stay dry underneath the umbrella of the canopy drip-line. Watching the water stain seeping slowly down the trunk is a very relaxing experience. Inching toward the ground, it soothes the parched chunks of bark, staining them dark with refreshment.

I counted the gap between the flashes of lightning and the claps of thunder. At two, I was a bit nervous about sitting in my car. The rain, as they say back in Scotland, was "stoating aff" the ground. Through the open window I could hear it hissing, soaking my left side. As I slapped on a good coating of sunblock, I could hardly see beyond the end of the car. The loud hammering on the roof reminded me of rain on a tent, and yet another camping trip about to go wrong.

When there was a nine- or ten-second gap, I was feeling much easier, knowing the toughest part of the downpour was over. Even the trees looked more relaxed. Everything outside had a much more subdued air to it. The sky was beginning to lighten and the wind was dying. A few red-winged blackbirds were making an attempt at getting things back to normal by squawking at each other—through the shortsightedness of the human eye, for no apparent reason. On the overhead wires along the roadside, one or two mourning doves had begun to settle, their soft *coo-coo-coo* just audible over the rustling branches. A crow was drifting by, slowly scouring the ground for anything the rain and the chemicals had flushed out onto the road. The raindrops were almost coming straight down.

When the count between the lightning and the thunder reached nineteen, the wind was gone. The rain was letting up, but the drops hitting the car sounded heavier, having put on a little weight by tumbling down from the topmost branches. Tree leaves are like vertical dominoes. The top ones overload, spilling their contents onto those below. The movement of the leaves is like a giant, slow-motion waterfall—each one tripping the next, tripping the next, tripping the next, cascading down the height of the tree into the tall grasses below. The water loads and unloads on the heads of the long thin stems. Their movement, unlike the uniformity of the tree leaves, is random. They do not ripple like a carpet of sprouting winter wheat in a breeze. They are a million swaying metronomes, a kaleidoscope of movement, each slightly out of synchronization with the others.

It was still raining when I stepped out of the car, wearing my T-shirt and waders. With my rain gear safely stored in the trunk, I grabbed my bag from the passenger seat, frisked myself—the Kirkland incident—searching for the car keys, found them through my waders in the back pocket of my jeans, rolled up the window and shut the door.

Stepping into the drizzle, I closed my eyes and drew in a long deep breath, tasting the woods, feeling the grass and smell of the earth as the air worked its way deep into my alveoli. *Boom!* An instant pleasure rush down the hot line to the pleasuredome in the brain. It's not a high; it is feeling the sublime, in a pure and natural state, and it is absolutely amazing. Sadly it is available only for a few precious moments, just as the rain is settling down, when the foliage is saturated and Nature hasn't fully got it in gear. Part of it is the silence. The great outdoors is a very noisy place, should you take the time to listen. But, here in the forced quietness behind the rainstorm, there are a few magical moments to savor—when the feathered territory disputes have, due to the rain delay, been postponed—and the squirrels aren't bitching at each other—or some parental bird isn't going ballistic because you're a wee bit too close to a hidden nest. There is, as the Druids said, "great power in silence." What would fly-fishing be without the time to enjoy moments like these? Not much.

I dug my baseball cap out of my bag, snuggled it down onto my head and adjusted the peak to keep the rain off my glasses. Under the uniform painting of the rain, the road, the gravel I was standing on and the riverbank were a continuation of each other. When development and Nature truly blend together, harsh edges and straight lines are softened beneath the sympathetic caress of a shower.

I grabbed my rod. The cork handle was still dry. I turned to check that the lights were off in the car—a great habit to get into—readjusted my cap and set off toward the trail leading to the river. Flash ... count to twenty-one ... *boom*, safe enough.

From the top of the trail, the path to the river doesn't look all that steep. Halfway down, it is quite another matter. The path is well used by hikers and mountain-bike folk, so there is little in the way of plant life sprouting on it. The topsoil has been long since washed away, leaving the clay base exposed to the elements. If that element happens to be rain, the trail becomes treacherous. Those of us with a sick sense of humor like the excitement of watching the bike lads scooting along it until they realize they are gonners. Even with the brakes locked, they continue to plummet towards the base of the trail. I, too, have skied down it on more than one occasion, and it is a bit of a thrill. Just after a downpour, only the foolish would chance it.

Contemplating my next move, I was picking out a route down through the bushes and trees to the side of the bike tracks. The path looked like a long ribbon of caramel, glistening from the water, as slick as puppy poop. Two steps later, I discovered a flaw in my plan and was plummeting toward the base of the trail, trying as best as humanly possible to remain in an upright position. Things were going "not too badly," until I hit a tree root and continued down the last 30 feet, face first.

Having gone through things like this *many* times before, I held the rod up to avoid any breakages. As soon as I stopped moving, I stood up and looked around to see if anyone had witnessed my wee bit of misfortune. I did this knowing full well I was the only one for miles around. We are a funny lot. I made a note to take the long way back up to the car park and to keep an eye out for cyclists.

I checked the rod for cracks, checked the waders for tears, checked the trail for wayward fly boxes—escapees from my bag—then checked to see if I was bleeding. Negative on all four counts, so I continued onward. My arms, shirt and the front of my waders were covered in mud, but that would wash off at the river. So, there I was, my gear dumped on the bank, washing out my shirt in the river. I felt like I was on some type of pilgrimage.

Here the river is beautiful, slow moving and meandering. The water is clear, although it has a green tinge, a reflection of the algae growth on the pebbles below the surface. It averages out at 2 feet deep, with pools that drop off to 4 or 5 feet. It is about 30 yards wide, but the floodplain reaches 200 yards in places giving the river a much grander status than it actually has. It has a very open and airy feel to it. Most of the riverbed is pebbled free-stone and there are large headstone-sized boulders freckled throughout the course of the river.

At this time of the year, the banks along the slower backwashes are thick with lizard's tail (*Saururus cernuus*). The tiny white flowers at the top of the stem form a spike about the same size as a pen, which is always drooped and curled over—hence the name. The flowers have a sweet fragrance: a mix of hyacinth and hazelnut. On some banks they form a spectacular border 3 to 10 feet wide. A word of caution about these plants: nine times out of ten there are stinging nettles growing behind them. The nettles can reach 5 feet tall and form thick clumps. When you are looking for a short-cut out of the river, it is *never* a good idea to blaze a trail through the lizard's tails, especially if you are wearing a short-sleeve shirt and the light is waning. By the time you discover the nettles, it will be far too late. Plus, it is almost sacrilegious to trample through such a pretty border of flowers.

With the waders washed off and the shirt back on, I picked up my gear and toddled some 300 yards down the bank to the head of the first set of rapids. In the summer, when the water is over 70 degrees Fahrenheit, there is no point in looking for smallmouth bass in the deeper slower pools where you *think* they would be, skulking in the shade and shadows. No, they like to stack up in fast-flowing, foamy, broken water. Maybe it is the extra oxygen being bubbled into the water that draws them. Or, maybe it's because they feel as if they are floating in a mini Jacuzzi. Who knows? Generally, during the hottest part of the summer, where there are bubbles galore, the smallmouth won't be too far away.

Not more than a foot or so from the bank of the river, carp were tailing in the shallows. By cleverly wearing camouflage colors—green and mud—I could get very close without spooking them. It was easy to see their tails poking out of the water as they rooted around, sucking up insects and crayfish from the riverbed. A few of the tails and fins had a reddish tinge to them. These belonged to some of the hardest fish to catch in Ontario—the redhorses.

I've seen thousands of these fish, staggering numbers of them, carpeting the river during their spring spawning runs. I've thrown hundreds of patterns at them. Not a sausage. Not even a "Thanks for coming out" hit. They are very tough to tempt. Had it been the same biomass of trout or salmon, there would have been hit after hit after hit.

Redhorse, hog suckers, gizzard shad, gar pike and the elusive quillback carp sucker may be the last of our truly wild species. Just about every other game fish has at some point been stocked; therefore, it is fair to say there is no way of knowing if the fish you just landed had hatcherial ancestry in some part of the family tree. (I just thought I'd include that a little tidbit for some of the purists to get worked up over. And while I'm at it, take a look at Lake Ontario, the World's Biggest Stocked Pond.)

Hidden behind a clump of purple loostrife, I stood content in the drizzle and I watched the fishy activity for about an hour. It was the same old same old. Fish eating bugs, fish chasing minnows, fish chasing each other and fish scooting for cover when the shadows of the circling seagulls crossed their path. "Looking for something to do," a pod of juvenile smallmouth bass were aimlessly milling around in a small depression in the riverbed.

The highlight in the aquarium before me was a black carp. As these are few and far between, I could not resist seeing what it was up to. It did exactly as the others were doing.

I've never had a black carp take a fly, and thought of them as being a variation of the common carp, something like a mirror carp. They are not. Black carp are blind. I've seen them up to about 10 pounds, so it just goes to show you how efficient their other senses are at sourcing food. Fish can change their skin pigments to help them blend into the background, and they do it by adapting to the colors being picked up through their eyes. Seeing no light or color, the blind fish thinks its surroundings are black, and changes to blend in with its perception of its environment.

In the clear, shallow water, catching either the redhorse or the carp is virtually impossible without the aid of a heavy downpour. In a foot or so of water, and with an unbroken surface, they are more difficult than usual to hook on a flyrod. Most other species of fish could take a lesson from these guys on being selective. If I wanted to get them, I had to wait until the heavens opened back up. The harder the rain fell, the more likely the carp were to bite. By the looks of things, the next cell of weather would be about an hour or so away. It was still raining, but the heavy drops were letting up quite quickly. As I stepped into the river, all the fish disappeared in a rash of mud trails and I waded out to the top inside edge of the riffle.

No sooner had I stepped into the river than the rain stopped. Everything around me seemed refreshed. The large boulders dotting the river had been transformed from white-gray blobs that looked like headstones and didn't belong there, into rich browns and greens, blending in with the river and the surrounding vegetation. The birds were having a go at each other, and I could hear the squirrels chasing each other in the trees. There were mayflies and caddisflies flittering about, but still there were no butterflies. It was a little bit early in the day for them. Usually they show up around nine o' clock, when the air has warmed up a wee bit, just as the first rays of sun hit the streamside vegetation.

I was soaked and slightly chilled, but that, too, would change when the sun got rolling, in between the thunderstorms. There had been just enough rain to soak my hat. Soon I'd be suffering from hot-head as the water evaporated in the sun. There was a gust of wind, and the last wave of rain dropped down onto the river.

I unhooked the Spike and sent it drifting down the inside edge of the riffle. It traveled about 4 feet when it disappeared in a swirl. Waiting until I felt the weight of the fish, I lifted into a smallmouth of about a pound. It cleared the water and threw the hook. Resisting the angling urge to pick up and recast, I let the fly continue down the drift. Seconds later, there was a smaller swirl and again the fly disappeared. I waited, then lifted. Without having to see it, the short, sharp tug-tug-tug-tug-tug told me I'd hooked a rock bass. The fish turned out to be no more than 5 inches long and there was an inch and a half of fishing fly dangling from its mouth. "Aggressive little buggers," I mumbled as I let it go. Chuckling—I love their "You wanna a piece of me" attitude—I worked some silicon floatant into the fly.

Just as I was about to recast, the sun poked through the clouds. It was a switch that turned on the river. More seagulls arrived; a few turkey vultures appeared out of nowhere, soaring on invisible air currents further downstream; and the songbirds got fired up. I could hear the unmistakable *Chick-a-dee-dee-dee-dee-dee* notes of a chickadee coming from the barren branches of a dead maple. He probably was nesting in an unused woodpecker hole somewhere in one of the limbs. From out of nowhere there were the buzzing and humming sounds of insects. Instantly, through my wet shirt, I could feel the temperature changing.

I snipped the Spike from the line and tied on an a size-6 Outcast Crayfish. The Spike would still catch fish, but there was no fun in watching it drift along the surface without a melody of raindrops and circles to accompany it.

For close to an hour (a guess, because I never wear a watch), I was doing well, catching a mix of smallmouth and rock bass: nothing big—most of the smallmouth were in the 10-inch range. The sun had dried out my shirt and hat. The big boulders were bleached again, and the butterflies—mostly cabbage whites with the occasional swallowtail—had finally shown up. Seeing butterflies or big fuzzy bumblebees always makes me smile. Even the cabbage white (*Pieris rapae*), small and lacking a coat of many colors like its cousins have, are a delight to watch, especially when a bunch of males—one black spot on their wings—climb a spiral staircase in pursuit of a female—two black spots on her wings—high above the trees on a mating flight.

Undisturbed, I'd settled into a fluid rhythm and was perfectly in tune with most of what was going on around me; therefore, hooking a lot of fish—the river will tell you where the fish are, if you let it and are willing to listen.

Distant voices drifted downstream from far above the bend. I couldn't see them but guessed two bass fishermen. They were wading, and from the hoots and hollers they were on opposite sides of the river, and my feeling of belonging to the river was instantly shattered. I pulled in the fly, cut it off and pinched a small split shot to the line, then began recasting. I've taken lots of 2- and 3-pound smallmouth from this part of the river, from water that looks like it holds nothing but boulders. By fishing without a fly, there was no way I would inadvertently let the cat out of the bag when the anglers showed up. Luckily, the next nasty bit of weather was about fifteen minutes away and I hoped it

would drive them off the river. The stormy sky was darkening quite nicely, the gusts were colder and the butterflies were fast disappearing. By the looks of things it was shaping up to be a good one.

The fishermen rounded the bend, one on each side of the river, chucking 6-inch lures into 6-inch-deep water. One hollered down to me, "Hey, you gettin' any?"

I put on my best poker face. "Nah! It's the first time I've fished here. Been here since before it got light. All I've got are some rock bass. What else is in here?"

"Smallies and pike." As he answered I noticed that the right side of his black T-shirt, emblazoned with a beer logo, had a large mud stain on it. It continued down the side of his waders, ending at the water surface.

"You lads gettin' any?" I asked, thinking, "What about the largemouth, mirror carp, redhorse, hogsuckers, carp, white bass, gizzard shad, rockbass, perch and the hornyhead, creek or river chubs?"

"Nothing. We haven't had a bite."

I pointed to the sky. "Man, this storm looks

worse than the one that rolled through this morning. I got soaked. Those cold fronts really put the fish down." Neither of these lads was wearing rain gear, and they looked like the type of folk who didn't like getting wet. I was now dumping my casts and slapping the line behind me.

I was too far away to hear what they were saying, so I continued beating the water to a froth. One chap waded across to his buddy. As they were leaving, heading to the base of the ski jump—somehow it never crossed my mind to tell them about the other route—he shouted down to me, "Hope ya have some luck." I thanked him with a wave and mumbled to myself, "I just did."

I have, over the years, been heavily influenced by the killdeer. By the time they were out of sight, I'd pulled off the split shot and retied the Spike onto my leader.

I could see the curtain of rain moving rapidly upriver toward me. There was no thunder, but the wind was more violent than it had been during the earlier storm. "Things are about to get very, very exciting, " I said to myself. Within minutes the water was dancing under the pounding raindrops; the tombstone boulders had once again become dark; crystal droplets were forming on the lip of my baseball cap, swelling, then dropping off into the river. I was soaked to the skin and loving every second of it. Without water, there is no life. Standing in the river, cloaked in raindrops, when there is no tension and no hurry, is for a brief moment an ideal way to get back to where it all began.

Throwing the line into the face of a storm cell is great for working on the casting stroke. If the forward line loop you are throwing is not tight, rest assured you're gonna be wearing or eating the line at some point. Is the practice worth it? Absolutely! Embrace the wind, for it is the fly-fisherman's best ally. That is, if the storm doesn't zap you and you don't throw out your back or put a tear in the muscular tendenous junction of your rotator cuff heaving the line around. Practice casting into the wind, and the next time you're fishing in a woosie-wind, one that has gleefully driven most other anglers—weather weenies—off the river, you can continue on in complete isolation, while they are whimpering and whining back at the car park. Remember, it is far easier to cast directly into the wind during your forward cast than to have the wind coming from over your shoulder when you're trying to aerialise the line behind you in a backcast. By the way, when you're casting, if your line loops are wide enough to drive a bus through, you're snookered no matter which direction the wind is coming from.

No fish were showing when I sent the Spike down through the riffles. Floating on the surface, being bounced around by the wind and surrounded by the splattering circles of the rain, the fly looked like it, too, was enjoying itself. Nothing.

"Odd. They should be all over this." Two more drifts. Nothing, then the lightbulb went on. I threw the fly outside the riffles, into an area of water no more than 8 inches deep, in front of one of the tombstones. It all happened at the same time. The fly just touched the water and a 2-pound smallmouth met it on the way up. As it

landed, it set the hook all by itself, as I was too shocked to do much of anything other than gawk.

Like the carp, the smallmouth had moved into very shallow water when the surface began getting pummeled by the rain. Here, they would take a whole host of patterns, like Freestone Nymphs, Bumbles, Smushed Hoppers or a Fuzzy Wuzzy, provided I fished them very, very slowly. I knew this, but sometimes things just slip away.

The storm lasted for almost an hour. By the time it ended, I had hooked countless fish, and the rain had wicked its way down past my shirt, soaking my jeans almost to my socks. My glasses had fogged up and I was looking through the streaks on the lenses. There was so much water cascading from the front of my cap I felt like I was in a monsoon. I loved every second and I wouldn't have traded a heartbeat of it for the world. All of the fish were hooked in the shallows, on the Spike, and without my having to move around in the water. When the rain is battering the river, everything below the surface becomes obscured, and switching from one spot to another is a foolish, and a dangerous, thing to do.

By the time the next front hit, my shirt had completely dried off. I'm always amazed at how hot the inside of a baseball cap becomes when the sun is drying it out. This weather cell was the weakest of the three, and I fished for carp through the whole storm, using an Outcast Crayfish, size 6. The fish were so close to the bank that I had to cast the fly onto the streamside boulders, then pull it into the water, to avoid spooking them. Over the years I've hooked hundreds of carp, and most of them head downriver. In a heavy rain, however, with few exceptions, they all run straight upstream. Very strange indeed. Few parts of the angling experience can compare with watching the line melting off the reel when you're soaked to the skin and you can't see through the condensation in your glasses. It is edge-of-the-seat intense and absolutely thrilling stuff.

All good things must end, and sensing that this had been the last thunder cell, I started up the trail, taking a detour to avoid another ride on the up escalator of mud. This path, if you could call it that, of flattened grass was no wider than its primary pedestrians, bunnies and groundhogs. It was easy to miss it at the river and almost impossible to follow as it wound its way out of the floodplain and through the bluff of willows, hawthorns and poplars toward higher ground.

Nature was drying out for the third time that day, and many of the large river headstones were once more becoming white. The birds were letting their voices be heard, the butterflies were skipping through the air, and an osprey was scanning the river, looking for an afternoon snack. Everything had the "fresh out the wrapper" feel to it, as I struggled through some of the dense vegetation overhanging the path. Thoroughly soaked and thoroughly contented, I was on top of the world, watching the trail, looking for shrews or scurrying chipmunks. Then, something I had never seen before stopped me in my tracks.

On the path in front of me was a white, flat, oval-shaped stone about 5 inches by 7 inches. On it, perfectly centered and framed by the edges of the stone, was a mourning-cloak butterfly

(*Nymphalis antiopa*) with its wings open, using the stone as a heat-sink. The dark maroon wings—about 3 inches wide—were splattered with a few iridescent blue spots and framed with ragged edges of pale straw yellow. There was only one dry rock on the path, and this insect had found it. Everything around it was a mix of browns and greens, the colors of the still-damp earth. Illuminated by a sun spot and through the tufts of timothy grass, the rock was almost obscured and would have been very easy to miss. In silence, I studied it for several minutes. It was perfect. I backtracked along the path for almost 10 yards, then busted a swath through some vines, nettles, poison ivy and only God knows what else, circumventing the butterfly. Something that perfect and that beautiful should always remain undisturbed.

When I eventually reached the car, two very spiffy lads—decked out in Spandex and sporting very trendy-looking sunglasses—were unloading a pair of very clean, spiffy mountain bikes from the back of a very clean, spiffy sport utility. We exchanged pleasantries.

"Did you get anything?" one of the cyclists inquired.

"Nah. A few rock bass."

"I've been fly fishing since the spring," he said, checking the spokes on a wheel.

"Oh yeah, in here?" I asked, breaking down my flyrod, hoping he might reveal a spot I'd never fished before.

"No, I go to Shellies Trout Ponds and Sweetpeas Produce, on the fifth concession."

"You get a few, do you?" I was disappointed, but it's always worth a try.

"Tons. There's nothing to fly-fishing. It's really simple."

"Yeah, so they tell me. I've only been at it for a week or two. I guess it's like riding a bike," I said.

Nodding in agreement, he threw his leg over the saddle and they both checked their handy-dandy wristwatches. "Yi'll no be needin' those, laddie," I thought to myself. "Stick with it, you'll get the hang of it," he said, pointing a remote at the car, locking the doors and arming the alarm.

They circled the parking lot a few times, to

warm up, I assumed. He gave me a cheery over the shoulder wave, then they shot onto the bike trail—at quite a good clip—disappearing into the bush. Above the happy *Chick-a-dee-dee-dee-dee-dee* liltings and the hurried rustling of a chipmunk in the long grass *en route* to a green garbage drum, I could hear the yelling and banging, and the sweet, wonderful sounds of carnage.

"Nice to know we've something else in common."

I unlocked the driver's door, slid my gear onto the passenger seat and hopped in still wearing my waders, the outsides of which were drier than the jeans inside. Backing up the car, all I could think was, "Stick with it, lads, you'll get the hang of it."

Bass and the Blond

This Thursday night happened to be the hottest of the year, and the summer bass season was less than a week old. Half-asleep and half-baking, I was basting on top of the bedsheets, listening to the neighbor's wind chimes and waiting for the thunderstorm, which was threatening the trees on every gust, to arrive and break the humidity.

Over the airwaves of my clock radio, I'd come to despise "Desperate Dave the forecaster" with his cheery voice and upbeat attitude of "There's a tropical front stuck over Southern Ontario. Nighttime lows should be around 28 degrees Centigrade, with a relative humidity of 55 percent. Tomorrow it will be hot, hazy and humid, with a daytime high of 32. With the humidex, it will feel more like 40 degrees, and a relative humidity of 70 percent. Expect the next few days to be continually muggy."

"Muggy," I muttered under my breath at him, "Muggy! I'll give you muggy. And *relative* to what? He's talking about his extended family when its 80-odd degrees Fahrenheit out there? Oh, I can't wait till tomorrow, when it hits 100!" I could have switched the air conditioner on, but I've always considered using one as somehow unnatural. As the wooden floors anticipated the storm, I listened to the rhythm of the creaking house and imagined the beads of sweat screaming "Wheeee!" racing each other down the toboggan slopes of my skin to the sheets.

Playing games with the bright orange numbers of the light-emitting diode display on the digital clock face, I proved conclusively to myself that time is fragile and a very personal thing. If I mentally moved the vertical bar from the top left side of the 5 to the right, I now had a 3. Where had the time gone and how had the shift affected me? Hardly the stuff of the Philadelphia experiment, but it beat the heck out of counting sheep. I pondered numbers. Is 0 obese, 1 anorexic and 8 a constant subliminal image of Frosty the Snowman?

At exactly 1:00 a.m. the phone rang, thankfully pulling me away from my numerical nightmare. A voluptuous voice, as sultry as the night I was in, whispered, "Are you alone?"

"Yeah." I rolled onto my side and focused on the receiver.

"Are you naked?"

I thought: who in their right mind, or out of it, would be wearing anything other than a birthday suit on a night like this? Then I answered: "Yeah."

Using only six words, she had my full and undivided attention. It was hard to imagine a woman getting a man to take notice with fewer words, but suddenly, "Honey, I'm pregnant" or "This fell off the car" sprang to mind.

She continued with: "My ex has the kids. I've the cottage and the island to myself for the weekend."

"A-ha?" I said, praying it wasn't a wrong number, but, then again ...

"If you leave now, you can be at the marina in four hours."

"A-ha?" I was off the bed, slipping into a pair of shorts but holding off on pulling on a T-shirt, which would require that I take the phone away from my ear, just in case I missed something good.

"We'll be rolling around naked in the sun porch by the time the mist lifts."

"A-ha?" I cursed myself for having a rotary phone and not one of those slick portable units—the ones that would give me the freedom to do a million important things while listening to some market-research group ask if I prefer waxed or unwaxed dental floss. Now, if I had one, I'd have the power to close a billion-dollar deal standing in a lineup for a coffee and a donut.

"Roam phones," like air conditioners and degrees Centigrade, might be the work of the devil, but, with a mobile unit, I could, by now, be in the car instead of tethered to a wall jack. I'd instinctively mapped out the shortest route through the house for scooping up fishing gear, a toothbrush and swim trunks, and loading snackies, with a bottle of my favorite fifteen-year-old single malt, into the trunk of the car. All of this done in a time that would make an Indi 500 pit crew spin. The last thing she said above the background of a calling whippoorwill was, "I'll expect you there at five."

"A-ha."

The click and the dial tone were seconds behind me as I backed out of the driveway, nursing a self-inflicted "rug burn" from scrambling into a T-shirt.

The four-hour drive north to Muskoka was uneventful. The sonic "Scare Away Critter" whistles on the car roof had done their job, terrorizing the local wildlife into staying well clear as I drove past. My route was 100 percent large-animal free, and without having to deal with a deceased deer or a mangled moose I made good time. Then again, if the whistle's high-pitched whines are well above the frequency audible to the human ear, how did I know they were working? It might have been that God's little woodland creatures were at a "must attend" function thrown by Mother Nature—the real reason I didn't see any. The drive was spent nurturing the anticipation of the morning after, from the passionate point of view of the night before. Soon we'd both be squirreling the images away for future fantasies.

Reaching the marina, I thanked the Creator for the peaking sexual drive of a mid-forties woman, fifteen years my elder, who knows what she wants and who walks a direct and confident path. She had a "show me" attitude with the kind of lust that can't be faked. With her there was no safety net—it was all or nothing, with little in the way of a gap between her aspirations and achievements. However, her insatiable Scorpian sexuality was not the only thing peaking. The cosmic souls of the heavens had aligned and bestowed upon the angler some of the best bass fishing within living memory. And here I was—"Oh, pity me"—about to head out onto one of the most productive bass fisheries in Canada, sharing an island with an incredibly luxurious lover and the type of woman most men don't even dare dream about. Very soon we'd be swept up in the headlong rush toward the lofty cliffs of ecstasy. If I were to die on Monday, it would take the funeral home weeks to wipe the smile off my face.

We woke at three in the afternoon, shared a shower, toweled each other dry, eventually got dressed and snacked on cucumber sandwiches in the cool shade of the sun porch. In the bay window of her library, she opened a book, poured herself into a large leather chair and curled up.

Preparing for a wee bit of angling, I unpacked my fishing gear. On the way out, I stopped to kiss her and was engulfed by her arms. I ran my fingers behind her neck, deep into the thicket of still damp, waist-length, natural-blond hair. Her favorite perfume, and mine, greeted me like an old friend, and my heart wanted to stay. I closed my eyes and drew in a long, deep breath. She sensed my weakness.

As I feebly tried to free myself, she still clung to my neck, giving me the sad-eyed-puppy look. "Please stay. Please. I'm all alone in this big old house. Please don't go down to that nasty cold lake. I may never see you again. The sea is a cruel, cruel mistress. Please." Grinning from ear to ear, with an "I have what you want" look, she drew the tip of her tongue across her partially open lips. I made a valiant effort to break her grip.

"Must-go-bass-fish'n. Can't-stay. Can't-listen. Must-fend-off-Siren."

She smiled seductively, knowing she now had the upper hand. I'd begun thinking from below my waist and was in grave danger of having brought my fishing gear for nothing. She wouldn't let up; her exuberance escalated. "Wouldn't you rather stay and help me get over some of my erotic inhibitions?" She pleaded: "I'll do anything. Anything. Anything your heart or any other bit of you desires." I started thinking I could go bass fishing when I got home; after all, I knew each fish by name and I did have an obligation to give them a workout now and again.

"Anything?" I inquired, half toying with the notion of getting her to ferry me over to Muskrat Bay, an area completely void of all life forms closely resembling mammals, for a bit of pike fishing.

"Anything," she whispered, slowly adding: "I can be tricked." I knew I had to leave.

Searching to find her soul, I looked down into her blue-green eyes and whispered back, "My beautiful, beautiful nymphet." She batted her eyelashes like the wings of a hummingbird; I paused for effect.

"That's what you say to all your women."

Instantly her hands fell from my neck. I pulled back from her upcoming playful slap, knowing it might leave a mark. She came up short. Grinning, she said, "Pig!"

With an "I've never denied it," I stepped out onto the top of the two-tier deck, closed the screen door, blew her a theatrical kiss, bowed, then bounded down the thirty-nine steps—not *the* Thirty-Nine Steps—of gray, sun-bleached, well-worn wood to the dock and the boat house.

Using a small Mugwump pattern on my 4-weight rod, I fished inside and around the edges of the boat house. The rock bass were nothing short of suicidal, and I'd soon honed my hook-setting reflexes back up to lightning-speed levels, all the while hoping it had indeed been the drive or, at least the heat, that had worn me down.

Around six o'clock, I switched to a Big Joe's Crayfish and decided to turn my attention to the main event of the weekend, the smallmouth-bass fishing. During the day, bright sunlight had driven the bass into the deeper areas of the lake, making them quite inaccessible unless fished with a full sinking line and a Crunchy Caddis, drifted from a boat. "Hey! Fish have no eyelids, so how else are they gonna adjust to the light intensity in order to detect prey?" Sunglasses and a baseball cap are simply not an option. Now, however, with the fading light, they would be moving into the shallower areas to feed. Cautiously they'd be sneaking along at the edges of the island in search of crayfish, minnows and insects, unaware of the danger they had inadvertently put themselves into by cruising well within my casting range.

Like half of an upturned pomegranate on a dinner plate, the island rises from the water. It is lush and green, covered with cedar, pine and white birch, and thick with plants and wildlife. The only two cottages are obscured by the vegetation, and, from the water, the signs of human habitation are limited to the boat house at one end of the island and a Beaver floatplane tethered to a dock at the other. It is a private paradise nestled in an oasis of tranquility. Clustered at the waterline are thousands of smooth boulders, hidden 2 to 4 feet below the surface. These rocks, some of which are 8 to 10 feet tall, are covered in a film of algae, making them a nightmare to walk on. Wading on them is like stepping onto a box of basketballs slathered in cooking oil. There is no room for a backcast, so it is a case of dainty, delicate wading and roll-casting.

I stripped down to my trunks and slipped into a pair of neoprene wind-surfing booties, the soles of which I'd customized by gluing on strips of a pink and yellow rubberized, non-slip bath mat. Not exactly a runway fashion item or fodder for a book on footwear, but they did a great job of providing traction on the slippery submerged slopes.

Given that there was nothing to hang onto, or nothing to brace my feet against should I start to slide off into the depths, I kept my equipment to a minimum. A small box of flies and a set of needlenose pliers were attached to a rope and worn as a necklace. Bare-chested, I felt primal and tribal, with an uncontrollable urge to tackle an Amazonian anaconda or go mano-a-hogo with a herd of wild pigs, using a blow gun, deep in the Bornean jungles. I knew, however, that the only thing I'd be putting into my mouth was the rod handle, each time I had to swim back to the island after I fell in.

Cautiously, I teeter-tottered along the first boulder until my feet found a flat surface almost safe to stand on. I unhooked the Big Joe's Crayfish from its resting spot, hooked on a guide, worked out some line and laid out a nice long roll cast. The fly and a small bit of split shot disappeared with a plop. I dropped the rod tip and started to count down the fly. I hadn't gone far when the tip of the line moved, I lifted into the fish and a 2-pound smallmouth cleared the water. Quickly I played out the Canadian Shield Bronze Back, gently releasing it back into the water. Several casts later, one fish was the result of my efforts. This was nuts. Something was up.

Down south, before I left, I'd been "dragging out" fish from areas where I'd never previously found them. Here, in a lake with a massive population of undisturbed fish, I should be into one on every second cast. Under less than ideal conditions in the fall, I'd drifted through a howling storm, the rain driven horizontally by gale-force winds, and hooked fish after fish in the 3-pound mark. There were several bonus bass over 5 pounds, and, as you would expect in a book about fishing, a bigger one that got away. So, something was definitely up.

One glance skyward confirmed my suspicions. The sun was still too high and the fish still too far from shore, but by half-past-seven or so it should be just about perfect. There was no point in complaining about the lack of fish, for I truly love this time of the day. These are the hours to feed the soul, when the day snuggles down and the night stumbles from slumber. The soft light, the golden amber glow and the warm hues are nothing short of magical. It seeps into the skin and suddenly you don't care about the fish you haven't caught; being there, in the moments between the end of the day and the start of the bugs, is more than enough. As the sun fell lower, I started catching more fish. Soon I was up to one on every cast.

Smallmouth are aggressive little creatures, but they are not stupid; then again, I've yet to catch a smart one. Once upon a time, in the shallow waters of an early spring day, David, an ace fishing buddy, a.k.a. Mr. "If it's a fishing gadget I gotta have it on my vest," and I watched a crayfish and a smallmouth perform a well-choreographed underwater ballet. The crayfish, the size of a small lobster, was sitting atop a large submerged rock, sunning itself in the warm shallows. A 4-pound bass hovered beside the boulder. As soon as the fish moved in to scoop up the crayfish, the crustacean raised its claws and the bass backed off. The bass moved itself around to the side, and the crayfish did the same and ended up facing its opponent. For a perfect square dance, all we needed was a fiddler, with the lower half of his face hidden by a beard he'd been growing since kindergarten, to stomp it out and call it.

"Face your partner, do-see-do, turn around then back you go! Suck him up, then swim about. If he's got claws, just spit him out."

Each time the bass moved in, up went the claws. The bass circled and the crayfish turned with it. When the fish wasn't being aggressive, the crayfish sat motionless, basking in the warmth of the sun, one would assume. Nature is amazing. Here, in a small back bay of a large Canadian lake, sits a crayfish, wallowing in the output of a massive ball of fire a gazillion miles away. We watched the scene for over an hour before we realized the dock we were building wouldn't finish itself. Eventually the bass gave up and the crayfish slipped off into the depths to worry about other things, like U.V. exposure and tan lines.

I watched yet another smallmouth swim away, realizing I had just entered into fly-fishing prime time. The wind was gone and the fish were feeding with gay abandon, attacking the crayfish in a rude and destructive manner. The tired, limp air was slowly reviving, and Nature was putting on her last hurrah for the day. The loons were looning, the whippoorwills whipping, the swifts and swallows swooping, and the bats, as bats do best, were silently trying to stay out of the way of everything going on around them.

I heard the screen door open. "How's it going. Getting anything?"

"Yip. Two or three."

"There's chicken salad when you're ready to come up."

"Thanks!" Focused intently on what I was doing, I'd failed to notice I felt hungry and that I hadn't fallen in yet. I could hear her footsteps coming down the stairs.

She reached the bottom and, without turning around, I said, "Don't worry about the line. I'm roll casting, so it won't hit you."

"Good. I've brought you down a grapefruit juice with ice."

"Thanks."

I turned my head to make sure I wouldn't tag her with the line. There stood Aphrodite. No, Aphrodite could never have looked this good standing on the shore of Cyprus.

She was naked. She was beautiful. She was deliciously enchanting. I looked at her slowly, as if discovering her sex for the first time. Her hair hung down to well past her waist, covering her in a soft, blond veil. She carried a silver tray with a single item, the tall glass of juice. It was her fig leaf. She didn't say a word.

I was spellbound and speechless. Without taking her eyes from mine, she put down the tray. Straightening up, she pushed her long blond hair behind her head, exposing her neck and two pear-shaped silver earrings. I couldn't pull my eyes from hers. Standing up to my waist in water, gripping a flyrod, I felt like a fool, and she, in the long evening light, looked like a goddess. An angelic radiant presence and the very essence of femininity; the lover to end all lovers and far above the limits of any imagination. Above her heart, on her left breast, was a small royal blue teardrop, a permanent ink reminder of a lost love.

"Your earrings—they look like teardrops of silver against your soft skin."

Still she said nothing.

Stretching, with entwined fingers, she pushed her hands skyward, arching her back, bending like a sapling swaying to the licks of a warm breeze. She looked amazing and to this day I don't know why I started humming "Land of the silver birch ..."

She reached down, extending her hand, and I turned, moving toward her. I was one step from her fingers when I felt my booties giving way. I reached up, and, in a desperate grope for something, anything, solid, I lunged forward, but the life line she'd offered was gone. Painfully slowly, I started slipping backwards, fumbling with my flyrod. I knew I was toast, and I had indeed been lured in by one of Phorcys's daughters. Disappearing beneath the surface, the last thing I saw was the immense grin spreading across her face.

I resurfaced just in time to watch her, a disappearing ghost, heading up the stairs. Behind her flowed a waterfall of hair, as her laughter, mixing with the voices of the loons and whippoorwills, echoed across the lake.

The room was black and rich with the thick musk of sandalwood oil. Through the ceiling windows above the bed, I looked up into the heavens and the Milky Way. The sky was clogged with stars, as thick as the snows of a January blizzard. I glanced at the heavy Waterford tumbler of Scotch we had finished over dinner. The crystal fractured and cracked the moonlight, sending the shards scattering across the bedside table. Luckily, we shared the opinion that ice was for skating on and it had absolutely no place in a glass of single malt. Beside the glass on the nightstand, the clock radio read 1:00 a.m.

My left arm was under her head and she was snuggled into my chest. So that I wouldn't sneeze, destroying the ambience, I was gently removing some of her hair from my face with my right hand.

Without moving, under a large sigh, she said, "Can't sleep?"

"Nah."

"Aww, too bad!"

I gave her a gentle poke on the forehead. She chuckled.

Exhaling, I 'fessed up: "I wish I'd got a bigger bass. Didn't get anything over 3 pounds. Wouldn't mind a photo of the 6-pounder I got last year."

"You're obsessed."

"Only with your untamed, ravishing beauty, my love."

She moved her hand and I said, "Uncle."

Then, in one fluid movement, she rolled away from me, sat up, sparked a match, lit an oil lamp, and by the time the shadows had danced across the walls, the match was out and she was once again snuggled up.

"Wanna talk?"

"Nah."

"Go."

"What?"

"Go. I won't be pissed off."

"Sure?"

"Hey, at least you're not rolling over and going to sleep."

I kissed her, saying, "Thanks."

Instantly, I could feel the monster smallmouth, tight to the shoreline, smashing into the Zonkers. Trying not to seem too enthusiastic, I hit the floor running, closed the door behind me and headed further into the darkened cottage. So as not to wake her any more than she was, I squirmed into my clothing in the kitchen. Waxwear pants, neoprene booties, long-sleeve shirt and a bug jacket with the hood pulled over my wide-brimmed hat. I set the whole thing off with a pair of yellow rubber house-hold gloves, secured to the sleeves of the jacket around the wrists with a pair of elastic bands.

At this time of night, the mosquitoes and their blood-sucking buddies can be horrendous. When the sun goes down, they do settle down a bit, but by tromping around and disturbing them, I was asking for it. My setup might look like something from a quarantine lab, and it might be as hot as hell until I was wet-wading, but it was the only thing to get me back inside without having to donate several pints to the biting-bug blood bank. I finished off my outfit with a flash, camera, flashlight, measuring tape and—just in case it all went wrong—a whistle. Then I made a mental note to ask the Creator, should I ever have the opportunity to do so, just what the devil was he thinking when he put those tiny vampiric guys on the planet.

I stepped into the sun porch and looked around, thinking, "Guess I left my gear at the bottom of the stairs." As I passed through the screen door, onto the deck, it didn't take long for the bugs to show up. Halfway down the stairs, I was sweating profusely and the mesh around my head was thick with hungry, and now-frustrated, bugs. "Too bad. So sorry to disappoint you. I've been giving all season."

There was no gear on the bottom steps. Moving, I'd increased my heart rate, going through more respiration, which in turn produced more carbon dioxide and heat. It seemed like every bug in the neighborhood had zeroed in on me and I was covered in them. My gloves were now black, but there was no bloodletting. My rubber skin couldn't be penetrated by a prodding proboscis or the army of sharp, piercing mouth parts.

"Bloody rat's arse!" I said to myself. "Where in the name o' the wee man is my gear?" I retraced the evening's proceedings. I'd scrambled out, dumped the stuff and chased her into the cottage. Dinner, game of chess, then bed, or did I dump my gear at the top of the stairs? Maybe she moved it underneath one of the benches or into the sun room in case it got busted. Maybe she moved it into the boat house. I'm about a quarter of the way there, so I better check.

Slowly wandering along the dock, gazing deeply into the vast sweeping heavens of starry expanse, I was pondering my insignificance in the grand scheme of things when I triggered the boat-house security light. The powerful beam scored a direct hit on my light-sensitive night vision, dropping me to my knees. I could feel it searing my retinas, and hear the cracking and shattering of kneecaps as they hit the dock.

"Aw, Jeez-usss, what's next?"

Next, when I'd regained my sight, was a locked door.

"%@!#**!!!"

Retracing my steps along the deck, I limped back toward the stairs, dropping pounds of perspiration with every step. Through the bug entourage swarming around me, signaling a popularity I could do without, I could hear the bass splashing in the shallows. Little wakes, bulges and ripples scooting across the surface as they chased minnows, crayfish and soft, squiggly, tasty things.

Taunting me, they were. Knowing I was rodless and in a state of disarray, they were taking full advantage of the situation, twisting the knife with every splash, knowing I could only watch.

Fish can tell when the angler is weak. They can pick up on the smallest chinks in your armor and strike with lightning speed. Take ice fishing, for example. All day you are out there; it's thirty below, your eyeballs are freezing and you can't remember the last time you had feeling in any of your fingers. Not for one second have you taken your eyes from the tip of your rod. Then, the instant you turn away to try to defrost a sandwich from your jacket pocket, to avoid chipping a tooth over lunch, whammo! The rod disappears down the hole. T'da!

The noble fly fisherman is no different, for it happens on the trout stream too. You find the perfect spot, you know the fish are there, you have on the perfect fly. Drift after drift has produced nothing. But you are in the zone; if a fish farts near your fly, you're gonna know it. Then, however, the instant you notice the blue and white phlox growing on the riverbank or the martins skimming the surface, popping off mayflies ... Whammo! There is a mighty tug, but you miss the hook set because you're mentally meandering in the meadows. Who among us has not watched in horror as a favorite rod disappears out the back of the boat, at the exact instant you set it down to reach into the cooler for a pop.

These are the classics, and no angler, no matter how careful and attentive, will go through a lifetime of fishing being totally immune to them. Should one of the multinational drug cartels, not the Colombians but the pharmaceutical collectives, develop a vaccine for Stunned Angler Syndrome, I'll be the first to roll up my sleeve. When aquatically ambushed, the angler should seize the opportunity and leave. Experience has shown that: (1) You will not be able to get the rod back; (2) There will be no chance for some type of vindication as you won't be able to catch the fish that did it; (3) Something very, very bad is lurking just around the corner. These quirky little numbers do have an upside, in that they are always funniest when they happen to your fishing partner, especially when it is an "only hit of the day" type of situation.

Truly a right of passage, these "how I lost my pole" stories that are not often spoken about, should be completely denied in tackle-shop chit-chats and tactfully avoided when talking to the spouse. Everyone has a fish-less day now and again, but when she asks, "How was your day?" think of the ramifications should you answer, "Not bad. Didn't land any. Had on a few and lost the $1,600 custom rod you and the kids gave me for Father's

Day last year. Think I'll just nip upstairs and wash up before supper."

Looking out across the lake to where the canopy of stars and the black shimmering surface became one, I could hear the bass splashing around. They knew that I knew that they knew that I was out of ammo, and they were poking fun at me. I watched them sending up shower upon shower of fleeing minnows, and I wondered: where *had* I seen that recipe for barbecued bass on a bed of wild rice?

Sweat was stinging my eyes as I limped toward the staircase. My fall had shoveled gravel inside my kneecaps, but knowing my gear was around here someplace, I was determined to push on. "Raccoons. It must raccoons. Those pesky masked bandits. *They* have my gear." Never, never underestimate the power of those deviant fur balls. Once, on a camping trip, I'd left a wienie impaled on a stick on the grill. The campfire was well out. Around midnight a "crunchy-munchy" sound woke me. I popped my head out of the tent and there was Rocky. He was sitting on his bum, like a giant panda setting about a bamboo shoot. He had the stick in both paws and the base was trapped between his legs. I looked at him. He stopped eating and looked at me. With a "Knock yourself out there, little buddy," I zipped up the tent.

I was now semi-convinced that my missing gear was definitely the work of raccoons. I could just see them, sitting on the boulders at the far side of the island. "Hey, George, how's my backcast? Ya gotta love this new graphite weave in the blank. Look at the thread work. The guy that built this was a master. Think I should try a Cranefly, or should I stick with a streamer? See if he's got any fly floatant in that box, and, while you're at it, root around near the lily pads and fish me out another crayfish, will ya? I'm feeling kind of peckish." Ho, yes, with every step I could see myself in a Davy Crockett hat, with a matching pair of gloves for the winter. Then there was a hippo-like splash behind me.

Quickly I turned to see what it was, but my knees gave out. I lost my balance, groped for the edge of the stair railing, missed it and felt the sickening *crack* of the flyrod beneath my hand as I rolled down onto the deck and fell onto the large boulders at the side of the stairs.

I lay there for several minutes without moving. Gazing into the heavens, this time I was far too afraid to ask, "What's next?" It took quite some time to compose and convince myself that somehow it was all for the best. At least I'd found my rod. It was now a three-piece, instead of a two-piece, but at least I'd found it.

I climbed the stairs like a penguin. By the time I reached the top and got my gear off in the sun porch, I was "knackered." Stepping into the kitchen I inadvertently caught her in the act. She was standing next to the fridge in her birthday suit, sporting a sheepish grin, clutching a tub of double-chocolate-chip ice cream, a bowl and a spoon.

"I couldn't sleep" was followed by "You're back early. How was it, get any photos?"

She scooped out several large dollops, opened the door to the freezer compartment at the top of the fridge, reached in and replaced the tub, saying

"Oooh! Ooh, that's kind-a chilly."

"I noticed," I said, then gloomily added, "I've had slightly better days."

Her mission accomplished, she was heading back to the bedroom, but she stopped at the door, turned and looked at me.

"What?" I asked.

"Nothing. You know what they say, don't you?"

"No, but I've a feeling I'm gonna find out right shortly."

"Aw, poor Mr. Grumpy!" Grinning she disappeared into the bedroom, adding "A blond"—she paused for several seconds and, without a hint of sympathy, went on — "in your bed is worth two bass in the bay."

"What?"

The lamp went out. Carried on the smoke of the extinguished wick, from deep within the rectangular "black hole" in the log wall came "A blond in your bed is worth two bass in the bay." She'd just cross-checked me from behind and slammed me head-first into the end boards. I'd been victimized in the true spirit of the Glaswegian idiom

"Never punch a man when he's down ... kick him, it's a whole lot easier."

"I love you too, my little ice-cream bunny. You can forget that back rub I promised you. Hey, by the way, I hear calories count double at night! Did you know that? Especially chocolate chip. It's got something to do with the moon's gravitational pull."

"Yeah right! By the way, there's hardly enough for another bowl. The cork fell out of your single malt and it spilled all over my ice cream. I might sue for negligence."

"Noooo, lassie! No the chocolate chip! Vanilla, maybe, but nooo the chocolate chip. Never. Woman, have yi no shame?"

"Nope!"

All was lost, so I made a hasty retreat.

To the sounds of a contented woman chuckling from the bedroom, making loud and very deliberate scraping sounds of spoon on bowl, I hobbled toward the shower to make myself feel human again, thinking, *en route* through the kitchen, "Must call Boris, my chiropractor, to get my knees sorted out with some acupuncture, and, much more importantly, she might be right: she may have found the Holy Grail of angling. She could be on to something."

But, when the cool jets of water hit me, I gave my head a shake, thinking, "Nah!" Then I wondered just how bad my rod *was* busted.

The Worlds on Irish Loughs

Representing one's country at an international event is both a thrill and an honor. Seeing the red and white Maple Leaf fluttering from a flagpole is the stuff of goose bumps. In September 1995, I was part of Team Canada competing in the World Fly Fishing Championships on Lough Corrib and Lough Mask in County Mayo, Galway, Ireland. The event was to be fished using "Traditional Loch-Style" for brown trout, a technique I'd learned growing up on the waters of Scotland, and one that I use each fall and spring in Ontario. I was over the moon and terrified.

We'd be drift fishing from a boat, casting three flies, downwind, into the area of water the boat had not reached. There are two fishermen and a boatman. One fisherman sits in the bow and one in the stern. The boatman sits in the middle. He uses an oar, trailed over the upwind side of the boat, as a rudder. Loch-style is at its best in high swells, whitecaps, a good stiff breeze, overcast skies and a gentle rain. The loch-style fisherman fears flat calm, windless and sunny conditions just as Florence Nightingale feared a porous surface.

One of the most amazing parts of this style of fishing is as follows, and you have to see this to believe it. A fish swirls at your fly, you panic and set the hook into nothing. Providing you've not "pricked" the fish and it hasn't "felt" the hook, it's easy to catch. You pull the fly off the water into a backcast, then deliver it back to where the fish was. Whammo! Nine times out of ten, the fish will grab it. If the fish felt the hook, or you "faff about," making several false casts, it won't work. In one cast, you take the fly away, make the fish look for it, then give it back. Simple and very effective. It's been working for me in the Great Lakes since 1980.

On one of my last practice sessions on Georgian Bay, before I left for Scotland *en route* to Ireland, Jay—a fishaholic, a die-hard down-rigger man, a die-hard fly fisherman, and, when conditions dictate, a die-hard spin fisherman, who works in the time off he takes from fishing—and I were fishing our faces off under a cloudless August sky. Hardly a fish was moving, and Jay was making rumblings about switching over to down-rigging. "No way in the world a rainbow's gonna come up to a size-14 fly away out here." He was right. Six hours of fishing in flat calm water produced nothing.

However, Jay became an instant convert to loch-style when he hooked his first fish six weeks later. His boat, the *Maid Marilyn*, was drifting on 3-foot swells; it was blustery and overcast, with the air having a good nip to it. "This ain't gonna work. It's gonna be the same as it was the last time we were out here. Fishless in Seattle."

"Come on, Jay, this is perfect; hardly the same as the last time. Just keep stripping the flies in." About an hour later we were a mile off shore when a 5-pound rainbow broke the surface. Wedged in its jaw was a size-10 Dunkeld Dabbler. The fish was skipping across the wave tops, and, as line poured out from Jay's reel, he looked over. His face was as white as his knuckles as he gripped the cork. He had an "I'd like a bit of help, here, Chump" look around him.

"Keep the tip up. Keep him on your reel so you don't get tangled up in any of the junk sitting in the boat. Try and lead him around to the upwind side of the boat, then the boat and the waves will be working with you, not against you." I didn't know how much he heard, I didn't know how much had made sense, so I added, "Try and keep him away from the prop, 'cuz you know what's gonna happen there." He nodded. Eventually Jay slipped the fish along the side of the boat, pulled out the fly, and with a splash, it was gone.

The "Vomit Comet" made the flight from Glasgow to Dublin in record time. The short jaunt across the Irish Sea can be a bit on the rough side—hence the name. Luckily, this time the flight did little to enhance its flowery reputation. Waiting for the connection to take me to Galway, I sat in the departure area, watching the planes. Looking out at the green and white markings on the tails of the Aer Lingus aircraft left me in little doubt as to where I was. Canada has the maple leaf, Scotland the thistle, and the Irish a shamrock. Unlike the Glasgow or Heathrow airports, where it is difficult to tell where you are from the aircraft on the ground, "You're in Ireland" screams at you from the shamrocks, painted on just about every plane. Contrary to popular belief, the grass is not greener on the other side—it's greener in Ireland. Scotland is beautiful. The snow-capped mountains, the heather and the black waters of the lochs will take your breath away, but Ireland will steal your heart. Like magic, it begins when you arrive and it never leaves you. You'll always want to go back. Always.

Sitting in the recently refurbished lounge area, I could smell the odor of the new carpet filling the room. The area was half-full, business men in dark gray suits, jean-clad tourists in faded denim shirts and mothers with kids pulling them three ways at once. One mother turned to her child, "If you wake the baabby, so help me, Rebecca, yi'll be gettin' it." The offending red-haired, blue-eyed sprog let go of her mother's leg and peered into the pram that her beleaguered mother was pushing. "*Weissshiss*," squeaked out between her finger and her lips. "*Shhhhhiss*." I watched and smiled. She was eyeing up the coffee counter with its shiny gold and silver wrappers. Crawling under a set of chairs, her brother was making a break for it. "Git oot'a thir, ya wee monkey," was enough to reverse the tiny shoes and coverall-clad bum. Just before his head had cleared the edge of the chairs, he lifted it. A heavy "thunk" reverberated around the room and the seats vibrated. I waited for the howl. It never came. Then I realized why these lads are so tough on the rugby field. In high school, the first two things our Irish coach told us were: When you're on the ground, release the ball. If you hit a man and he gets up, you didn't hit him hard enough.

The wee one's mother knelt down beside him,

running her fingers through his hair. "Jesus, Mary and Joseph, yi might have hurt yirsell." Giving him a soothing mummy hug, she added something in Gaelic as he disappeared into the folds of her brown cable-knit sweater. He wrestled free as there was an announcement that the next flight out was for Sligo. Seeing—and seizing—the opportunity, his sister also made a break for it. Gently, and with a soothing smile, an all-knowing flight attendant captured them both. Hand in hand, the entourage headed through the loading doors. I pushed myself out of my big comfy seat and wandered into a coffee lineup. My loonies had been changed into Scottish pounds and those to Irish punts. The coins felt strange and heavy in my pocket, clue number 2 that I was in Ireland. Clue 3 was the lack of a condom dispenser in the washroom. I purchased a juice and went back to watching the comings and goings of the aircraft. Over the next hour, flights went out to Belfast, Cork and Manchester. "Manchester! Who in their right mind would want to go to Manchester?" I thought to myself. "Maybe a returning pack of marauding English football hooligans, fresh from a foray into Europe, but having staggered onto the wrong flight out of Frankfurt."

Galway was announced. I gathered up my bags and stepped through the doors onto the tarmac. It was a bit windier and warmer than I'd thought it would be. The whine of the jet engines and the dull hum of the prop aircraft plucked at my ears. My traveling companions and I boarded a green and white shuttle bus that would take us out to the green and white twin-engine plane. Galway was a hop, skip and a jump away.

I settled into a window seat, and soon we were droning above the silver shimmering loughs, the peat bogs and the lush green fields framed with gray dry-stane dykes, heading over the West of Ireland countryside. There were cottonball clouds around me and cottonball sheep below. Somewhere behind me, I could hear the members of the English team commenting and laughing. I tried not to listen, but couldn't prevent myself. They were confident. In the big scheme of things, these lads, the Welsh and the Irish, were the favorites.

Canadian hopes for world domination of fly fishing were best described as slim. Slap on the skates, freeze a few loughs and, instead of a Guinness, pull some pucks out of the fridge and, without question, the outcome would be different. A few crystal drops of rain crawled across the window. A double-overtime, come-from-behind win was not going to be an option for Team Canada. It was not looking good for the boys with the maple leaf logo on their jackets.

Ireland, Scotland, Wales and England are the cradles of fly fishing. The sport slipped and slithered from these wombs hundreds of years ago. It was also the birthplace of parliamentary democracy, curling, golf and, more recently, mad-cow disease, which must surely count for something. Some say it was the Egyptian pharaohs or the Macedonians who started fly fishing. If they did, they've not done much with it since. Britain is fly fishing's hallowed ground—or water. India and Pakistan have cricket, and they can keep it. The States has basketball and baseball, two of Canada's great exports, and Canada has lacrosse and hockey.

The U.K. has fly fishing, and I had a feeling it was about to prove it to the rest of the world.

"Please fasten your seat belts, and put your trays and seat into an upright position. In a few minutes we'll be starting our descent into Galway. Thank you for flying with Aer Lingus. If you're taking part in the fishing championships, good luck and welcome to Ireland"—silky-smooth, the voice wafted across the intercom. Then the message was repeated in Gaelic. She could have been reciting the obituary column from the *Irish Independent*, and it would have sounded as syrupy and sleepy. Hearing her bedroom voice was well worth the price of the airline ticket. Small cheers came up from various sections of the aircraft. These boys had either been eating lots of red meat or had high hopes of winning. A couple of minutes and a few bumps later, the plane stopped at the terminal. As the passengers struggled with coats and carry-on items, I watched the ground crew begin to unload the luggage. There was one trolley set aside for rod tubes and, by the looks of things, it wasn't going to take long to fill it. We disembarked.

The trolley of rod cases arrived inside the terminal, and with it I dismissed any notion of winning a medal. Some of the biggest names in the sport were collecting the cases. These were the chaps I'd seen in the monthly British angling magazines and newspapers. I pinched myself, wondering, "What the hell am I doing?" I picked up my rods and luggage, then headed for the exit. Outside it was raining, blowing and blustery. Three of the women from the flight crew were hanging around outside the sliding doors of the terminal. I couldn't help but wonder which one of these colleens had the golden voice. I thought of asking, then thought better of it. I wandered around until I found the taxi stand. An older-model, black Mercedes was at the front of the line. Oblivious to the rain drops, its driver was bent over polishing the hood.

"How much to Ballinrobe?" Not that I was in any position to negotiate the fee.

He quit rubbing, raised his head, eyed me up and down, and took note of my cache of rod tubes. "You fishin' at the Worlds?"

"Aye."

"Who fir?"

"Canada. I'm fishin' fir Canada." He picked up on my accent. "When'd the Scots start fishin' fir the Canadians?" He put the rag in his back pocket.

"Since I started living there, sixteen years ago. How much to Ballinrobe?"

"You from Glasgow?" I racked my brains to see if there had been any recent sports-fan skirmishes between the Scots and the Irish. I came up blank. "I grew up there." I had no idea where he was going, but I had to go along.

"Twenty punt."

"On or off the meter?"

"I canna see a meter runnin', can you?" My gear was tossed into the back seat. I handed him the money, slid onto the polished leather passenger seat, clicked closed my seatbelt, and off we went.

Irish roads were designed with a typical Irish sense of humor, the engineers having never once been acquainted with the concept behind a straight line. The light gray asphalt has more twists and turns than a ferret in a hutch full o' chubby bunnies. Adding to the roller-coaster ride, the hedges, shrubbery and dry-stane dykes are tight to the sides of the road. It's a bobsled run, where the sides are emerald green, not snowy white. Passenger-side mirrors on rental cars are scratched, shattered or busted off, the cornering skills of tourists being not as good as those of the locals. My driver could easily have been a contender at any speedway. The holy pictures glued to the dash, and the statue of the Virgin Mary, were obviously more than mere statements of religious belief. It didn't take long for me to realize he was prolonging the life of the car's breaking system by simply not using it. Careening through the countryside, much of it a blur, two things happened. I became reacquainted with my God, and the word "tranquility" never once occurred to me. During the drive north, along the T40, we talked about how Corrib and Mask were fishing, the severity of Canadian winters and whether or not I'd heard of his cousin living in Winnipeg.

We flew past exits for Muckrush, Annasghdown and Luimnagh, until we reached Headford, one of the towns where the headquarters of the championships was based, near Lough Corrib. Slowing the car, he pointed to a door with a faded Guinness sign above it. "See that pub?"

"Aye?"

"If you want ti know which flies tae use, ask in there." By the time I'd said, "Thanks," Headford was quickly disappearing through the back window. "Mind 'n' ask for Basil, Basil Shields. He's a hell o' a fisherman, a hell o' a fly tier an' a big fan o' the Claret Dabbler. His boat's oot o' Ardmasillagh, near Oughterard, oan the other side o' the lough."

"Basil it is." I hoped he'd now keep both eyes on the paved goat track, cleverly passing itself off as a road. Then I asked, "Can I mention your name?" He looked over. God, I wished he wouldn't do that, especially not at our current cruising speed. "You can if you want, but he diz'na know me fae Adam. I've heard he's a hell o' a fisherman aw the same." I nodded and braced myself for the last few miles.

Luckily the sign for Ballinrobe flew by, just as I ran out of prayers and deals with the Man Upstairs.

"Where you staying?"

"Lakeshore Holiday Homes in Cushlough. It's on Cahir Bay."

"I know fine where it is." I'm glad he did, because I hadn't a clue. "It's no far fae town. I took some o' the German team oot there. David Hall, the guy that owns it, fished for Ireland. He's better than Basil, but only on this lough. Mind you, Basil's better on Corrib, and David's better on Mask." Thankfully he slowed down to a speed better suited for this part of the road, now little wider than the car. Here, the hedges and brambles reach out into the road and, like giant Venus flytraps, wait patiently for cyclists or unwary sheep.

We pulled into the driveway of a well-kept, quaint cottage with a beautiful garden. Opening the car door, I was greeted by the soothing smell of flowers and the distinctive aroma of a peat fire. Stepping from the car, I entered silence, except for the rustling of trees and the twittering of birds. I pulled my gear from the back of the car, dumping it on the trimmed wet grass beside the driveway. Extending his hand, and a business card, he said, "There you go, lad, safe 'n' sound. If you need a lift back to the airport, gimmi a phone. Best a' luck. You'll be needin' it. Today was the only rain we've had in four weeks. The fish'll be awfully hard to get. It's the driest, hottest summer we've had in living memory. The loughs are doon aboot 10 feet." I shook his hand, and thanked him. Glancing at the card I expected it to read: "Archeon River Autos. Call Charon and save a few obolos on your next trip." As the car disappeared, I reflected that this was not the Ireland I remembered from my boyhood trips.

Ireland in September was waxwear pants and jackets; made-by-my-mum Arran sweaters; two pairs of socks; wellies; and rain. The train ride down through the coast of Scotland in the rain, the ferry crossing from Stranraer—through Loch Ryan and across the Irish Sea to Belfast—in the rain, fishing under dark gray skies, and the rain. The constant drizzle or the full-blown gales. That was my Ireland in September. Bobbing up and down in a 15-foot boat, with the angry, cold waves splashing over the bow. Being thrown around, trying to hang onto the seat but ending up rolling around in the bottom of the boat as it pitched and heaved in the swells. The constant, acrid smell of a badly tuned, spluttering outboard. The endless hum of the wind tugging and pulling at my hood. For a shore lunch of soggy sandwiches, I'd huddle under a tree, watching the waves tossing the tethered boat up and down. That was my Ireland in September; that was what I expected. Big waves, big winds, big rain storms and big, big browns. That was why I'd spent two full days rewaxing and repairing my rain gear before I left Ontario. That was why I'd bought a new pair of wellies for the boats. Judging from the cabbie's suntan, I was secretly thanking the "fishing guide hand of fate" that had thrown a bottle of SPF-30, waterproof sunscreen into the bottom of my suitcase, beside the three sweaters and two pairs of woollen fingerless gloves.

The crunchy pea-sized gravel ended at a wooden cottage door, on which was a note saying: "Ian, pick a bedroom that's not being used. The fridge is full. If you've got the time, tie up a some size-12 Murroughs and size-14 Green Peters. Back around six. Thanks." I pushed open the heavy door. It creaked and groaned. Inside, the cottage smelled of peat. It was warm, clean, dry and very cozy. On the walls hung framed faded newspaper clippings of "man with fish" photos. The coffee table was piled with tattered, well-thumbed fishing magazines, and newer, slick County Mayo tourism brochures. The kitchen table was awash in the feathers and furs of fly-tying. Obviously the lads on the team had been busy. From looking at the materials and the scraps in the garbage, it was clear that Green Peters and Bumbles were the order of the day.

I dumped my stuff, assembled my rods, two 10-footers and a 12, stuck them in the sun-bleached wooden rack outside the back door, and went for a walk. A hundred yards later, I was standing on the pebbled shore of Lough Mask and 20,000 acres of the best wild brown trout fishing in the world. As I stood, feasting on the beauty spreading out before me, "The gods must surely envy those who live here" sprang to mind. In the distance I could see a few small boats, drifting on the dark waves, with the occupants casting downwind. Bright yellow rain slickers stood out against the shadowy greens of the Artry mountains, the black boiling water and the gray pumice sky. I found a nice rock, sat on it, tightened up my rain hood and closed my eyes. Feeling the wind and the rain on my face, I was fifteen years old. Now, years and a continent later, I was going to fish for the land of my birth at the world championships. "The World Championships"—the words rattled around in my head. "The World Championships." One hundred and forty of the best fly fishermen in the world. "Oh Christ," I muttered into the breeze. Inhaling slowly and deeply, I let the cool air fill my lungs. I tasted the Atlantic and the Mountains of Mayo. "Jeezus," I said, exhaling and shaking my head. In silence, I let the picture before me flood my senses. An hour passed. I started up the mile walk, back to the phone box we'd whizzed past on the way in,

thinking, "Best call my da and let the folks back home know I got here safe and sound."

As I turned my back to the lough, little did I know that it would be over a week before I'd feel a good breeze, the rain, or the need to wear my inclement-weather clothing.

Team Canada spent a week in Ballinrobe before moving to Galway for two final days of practice. These guys were the best in the country. Very experienced on the world scene, all with impeccable angling credentials and the ability to pull fish from a bathtub. After three days of practice, we were yet to see a fish. After four days, we had a rise. Things were looking up, for, on the fifth day, we had a hit. Rumors were thick that most of the other teams were fishless. Little consolation when you're in a boat for eight hours without so much as a swirl or a glimpse of a fish rising. The week was sunny, and that, combined with the low water conditions, meant the fish had little choice but to go very deep—and that was very bad.

The fishing was brutal. This was an angling

beating we'd never forget. We were getting thumped, big time. This was waking up and not looking forward to eight hours of fishing, on one of the best waters in the world. This was wanting to go home and vacuum the mail box. On the sixth day, there was not a cloud in the sky and, without so much as a ripple on the water, things looked bleak. John, one of our boatmen who'd been born and raised at the lough, and who had fished it for over sixty years, summed it up best. As we exchanged "Good mornings" and loaded our stuff into his boat for another day of suntanning and good conversation—completely undisturbed or interrupted by a fish—we asked him how it looked. John shook his head. "Just a wee bit better than hopeless." He paused, looked skyward, rubbed a chaffed hand over three days' gray stubble, then added, "Hopeless." He adjusted his dark green baseball cap. Embroidered in gold thread, Ireland shimmered with the water under the morning sun. Moving beneath his hand, tufts of gray hair poked from the bottom of his cap. His steel-blue eyes, nestled into deep sockets, and the brown-etched

folds and furrows of his face said it all. Motioning for two Canadian hopefuls to get into his boat, he said nothing. We understood, and did his bidding.

Pulled by the long wooden oars, his boat slipped slowly through the gray boulders exposed by the summer drought. This was his boat. His lough. His fish. His pride. A killing disappointment clung to him. You could see it, and you could feel it, but you couldn't change it. Soon the lough loomed large before us. John flipped the oars into the boat. I watched the water running off the ends, dripping onto the sky-blue chipped and faded sides, then puddling on the floor. I wished the lough would give up one fish. One fish. The three of us knew that the thousands of fish John had caught over the years meant nothing.

Good guides are driven by a fierce pride. Pride, not in fishing prowess, but in the ability to put clients onto a fish, from the waters you understand, from the waters you call home. John was a man drowning in sight of shore, slipping further below the surface as each day passed. Offering him my hand would go unnoticed. In his position I'd do the same. A lough or river can be cruel and unforgiving, and Mask was being miserable. After sixty years the water turned on John, cutting him off and shutting him out from her secrets. Within a week, he knew her in name only. Every good guide knows this will inevitably happen. John pressed a button and the 10 h.p. engine, the largest allowed on the lough, burst into life. I finished tying the third fly to my leader and glanced at him standing at the stern, guiding us safely and methodically through the minefield of submerged boulders. Behind him, like the vapor trail of a jet, white bubbles streamed across the silver lough. Before him, I hoped the bow would find a fish. After eight hours of washing flies, it did not.

Each evening, after practice, the team would reflect on yet another day of baffling and utter frustration. This is paradise, breathtakingly beautiful, and an angling Garden of Eden. Tragically it seemed that we were all eating from the same barrel of apples. At one meeting, another boatman had told us, "Well, boys, shows you how honest the Irish are; not even the fish are on the take."

There was little doubt in the minds of those relentlessly flogging the water that he was right—at least about the fish.

On the nightly phone calls back home, my da, Mr. "Just because it's a serious issue, you don't have to take the issue seriously," was having all kinds of fun with our misfortunes. After hearing of our lack of success, between bouts of laughter he'd start into "Do yi want me tae send over worms or some baggie minnows? How about fax'n you a photo of a fish so yi'll know what you're tryin' to catch? Can the team no go tae a stocked pond tae build up some confidence? Guess ther's nae chance o' you bringin' back a few fresh brownies fir yir granda's supper. Have yi tried usin' Irish flies for Irish fish? How long have yi been a fishin' guide?" Then, before he'd hand the phone to my mother, he'd holler, "Hey, Agnes, it's *your* son on Team Fishless calling. *Your* eldest boy, numero uno. You know, the Canadian that canna catch Irish fish. I've only got one son, and he never fly fished in his life." I'd hear him laughing, handing her the receiver, then he'd add, "Ask him how the vacation's gauin' and how's his suntan? He'd be better off on the beach at Dunoon. Ask him if the team are gauin' on any boat cruises?" The warmth in his voice always made me smile. Under the stars, on the long walk back to the cottage, I'd think of his sarcastic and caustic comments, and my laughter would shatter the inky silence. Later, my bed seemed cozier as I drifted off to sleep.

The night before the final day of practice, the team made a group decision—only maple syrup is more Canadian—to split up for the final day. Some of the team would head north to Lough Carra, a smaller lough of about 4,000 acres, where the fish were, as the guides informed us, "willing to have a go," so they could play out an Irish trout. Tom, a teammate, and I would stay and flog Mask for another eight hours. If the fish turned on or, if by chance a pig flew by, we'd be there to see it. The following morning we wished the lads good luck and wandered down to the boat launch.

John was already at his boat. The great lough was flat, twinkling beneath a cloudless and pigless sky. "By the looks o' things, it's gonna be the same as yesterday," he said, securing the outboard to the back of the boat. When the season was open, he fished the lough every day. He knew the water. His hands and face were as weathered as his boat. He was a picture of credibility. Every one we mentioned his name to said he had an Irish second sight for fish. I'd always thought that the Irish second sight was reserved for leprechauns and the supernatural. This was the first I'd heard of it working for fish. Either way, John had a remarkable reputation. Fishing the lough was the bedrock of his life. Tom and I climbed into the boat. I asked the same question I'd asked every morning: "John, where d'you think the fish are?"

"I'm stumped. I've fished here fir more than sixty years an' I've never seen the likes o' this." There was a deep sadness in his voice. Shaking his head he added, "I truly don't know. It's desperate!" Someone suggested fishing over the deepest part of the lough. John agreed and began working the oars. Once more he nudged the bow through the smattering of boulders around the boat launch. As he worked the oars, he said, "I heard the Aussies caught a few fish near there, pullin' wee Claret Dabblers, Bumbles 'n' a Peter Ross, 'close in' at the back o' the island. Maybe they've shifted oot tae the deep channel. Nae doubt, we'll find oot when we git there. They'll no be many boats oot here the' day. Everyone's gone tae Lough Carra. How come you two are'na gauin' there?"

"Truth is, John, we're too lazy to drive ..." Tom cut me off with "And stubborn. Plus the competition's going to be here on Mask, not Carra. So there's no point in going up there, is there?" Never missing a stroke, John added, "Fir sure. Nae point tae that at'aw." As we cleared 'the minefield' and entered the main part of the lough, John started the outboard. Tom nodded from the bow and I secretly crossed my fingers, while scanning the sky for swine.

It was a long run down to the deepest part of Mask. The great lough was intimidating. John finally cut the engine and, in over 90 feet of water (he guessed), he and I traded places. "What we need's a wind. Any type of ripple will huad fish. I'll stick in baith oars, so we kin chase the wind if it ever comes up." John put the oars into the water; they hung limp, sticking to the sides of the boat. We searched the surface for any sign of a fish. Three hours passed and only the oars had stirred.

Small wisps of wind had crumpled the water, and we'd fished them. Nothing, not a rise, not a swirl, not a splash, nothing. The morning dragged. Lunch was eaten in silence. Taking a cue from the morning, the afternoon dragged. Convinced that we were right, we floated across the deepest part of the lough. Nothing. The sun was just starting its slow descent toward the mountains and evening. Tom was changing flies, and my 12-foot rod was starting to feel a bit on the heavy side. I handed John some of the flies from my box. "Will these work?"

"Aye, they'll work. But no' in here." These were desperate times, calling for desperate measures, and I was desperate.

John suggested using two dry flies: a big one on the bob, and a small one on the dropper. We both agreed the point fly should remain something small and silver. We had used this system before and it hadn't moved a fish. Still, I had to believe in his judgment. He pulled two rusty, beaten-up, seen-better-days flies from an old, round tobacco tin, said nothing and handed them to me.

I put the size-8 Claret Murrough on the bob and the size-10 Green Peter on the dropper. From my box I pulled out a size-14 Peter Ross, one size smaller than the one I had on the point, and switched them. I sharpened John's flies, greased them up and threw them out onto the water. On the flat, calm surface, the large dries looked like a pair of beach balls, conspicuous even at 25 yards from the boat. This was unorthodox. Polar opposite to what we should be fishing. That size of Murrough was for use in 4-foot swells on dark rainy days. Tom was in no hurry to finish tying up. A breeze tweaked at the surface, and a fish rose to the Murrough. I did the only decent thing I could and pulled the fly away from the fish. The tacky psych effect kicked in, and everything unfolded in slow motion.

All eyes were on the swirl some 20 yards from the boat. Telling myself not to panic, I pulled the line into a backcast. "Don't hurry, don't hurry, don't hurry, you've done this many times before," I said to myself. "Pull the fly away, then put it back. Pull the fly away, then put it back. Point your thumb at the fish and drop the fly on its nose." I felt the cast straighten out behind me, then carefully pushed the rod forward; the line unfurled and the flies landed within inches of where they should have. The Murrough floated onto the disturbance left by the fish. I braced myself for the hit. "Here we go, here we go. Grab it. Grab it," I said to myself. "Grab it!" The flies sat there. I braced. They sat. I braced, God, did I brace. All I needed to do was twitch the flies. I did. They twitched. The fish hammered the Murrough. "I knew it was going to do it. I knew it. I knew it. I knew it. Goddamn it, I knew it!" flashed through my mind. As the ripples widened, I felt the weight of the fish, struck into it and, as I did, realized I had done so a second too soon. The fish dove and, on the taut line, the fly slipped from its mouth.

I felt sick. I felt as if I'd backed over a puppy. I took off my glasses, closed my eyes and hid my face in my left hand. I could see the paws poking out from below the tire. I put the rod down and buried my face into both hands. Exhaling, I could feel my warm breath being pushed back onto my face. I could hear it echoing in the cup of my hands. I took a series of deep breaths, then dropped my head down onto the edge of the boat. The narrow strip of oak was hot against my forehead. I was hoping that one side of my body would go numb, preferably the left. Two days before the World Championships, this was exactly what I needed. Quite the confidence builder. I'd rather have taken a whack from a Canadian grade-1 two-by-four than miss that fish. If you're gonna get smacked, it might as well be from the best. Tonight, snuggling into my bed, this magical moment, this little angling gem, would be replayed in a never-ending nightmare. No amount of tossing and turning would erase it. On the VCR of deep-sleep torment, the pause button would be busted, and the stop button would be conveniently missing. The prospect of a good night's sleep was slim. I had no doubt as to what my da would say on the phone.

Massaging my eyeballs with my fingertips, I kept my eyes closed, hoping the darkness would consume me. Never in the history of my world was there a more perfect time for the grim reaper to make a guest appearance. A week of frustration, and now this. "And it just keeps getting better," I said to the lough. I could feel the phantom weight of the fish in my right arm. I couldn't control my laughter. Without lifting my head from the side of the boat, through my giggles, I stammered, "It took the Murrough. It took the bloody Murrough. It took the bloody Claret Murrough. Bloody Claret Murrough. Bloody hell. Bloody rat's arse. RAT'S ARSE!" I still had my head on the gunnel, when I heard John's Irish lilt, "Aye, that's a grand color for a Murrough in here." I was lost to laughter. It didn't take long for my boat partners to join in. Soon there were tears in our eyes and fishing was canceled due to our inability to look at each other without howling. The great lough had handed out a Halloween treat while I was hunting Easter eggs.

Later, when the boat was moored, the gear unloaded and the bottom of the orange sun pricked by the dark distant peaks, I thanked John for tolerating my inadequacy. He smiled a warm kindness, similar to that of the flight attendant who had rounded up the kids.

That evening, I called my da. Hearing the story, he rose to new heights and hit top form. On the mile walk back to the cottage from the phone box, beneath the constellations and the Milky Way, I could smell the heavy, sweet aroma of peat smoke. As Ralph McTell wondered in his lyrics, "Who scattered the stars in the fields of the night?" I walked through the warm blackness, looking up, but all the while keeping an eye out for the tendrilous brambles.

River Dusk

When I started this book, I never thought about how I was going to end it. I kind of figured nature would run its course, and it would, all by itself, somehow, just sort of happen one day. I'd open my "master text don't screw up" file and a little warning symbol would flash onto the screen of my Macintosh computer saying, "Error 77—You're done!"

As I worked on the manuscript, and the pile of coffee mugs around me steadily grew, I had many wonderful, witty endings—at least I thought they were—jotted down on various scraps of paper and empty pizza-delivery boxes. But none of them felt right, none of them had the comfort of the old, wornout T-shirt and pink, pig-print boxer shorts I wore when I wrote most of this. (What did you think I was wearing—my kilt?)

To clear my head—and I hoped, come up with something you, the reader, the person who matters most of all, would not find disappointing—I did what I do best: I went fishing. You've managed to stick it out this far, so you deserve—and rightly so—something more thoughtful and visual than a full stop.

It's mid-August, around seven in the evening; the cloudless sky is a deep azure color. Upstream, just below the treeline, there is a warm, orange haze. Here the river is 60 yards wide, sluggish and languid, like corn syrup on cold crepes. Looking upriver, to the right there is a steep bank rising up at about 70 degrees, covered in a thick bush of maples, cedars and willows. Bright yellow goldfinches, conspicuous against the lush green foliage, dot the streamside, like wild canaries, plucking at thistle seeds. I've missed more hits while watching these birds than I'd care to remember. To the left is the floodplain, an inpenetrable jungle of cucumber vines, nettles and head-height grass about 200 yards wide.

Towering above the blanketed undergrowth is a dead tree, stripped of bark and almost branchless. Riddled with holes, it looks like woodpecker central. On the top branch is an adult great horned owl. It is almost a silhouette, but the ear tufts are unmistakable. Two branches below is a fluffy down-covered immature owl. Great horneds will lay their eggs when the snow is on the ground, so this little chap is well on in its development. Compared with the majestic stature of the parent, the youngster is kind of goofy-looking, tottering on the limb below it. Its ear tufts have not sprouted, and with its head covered in thick, fluffy plumage, it looks like it's wearing a crash helmet, or one of the old leather flying hats from the open-cockpit days. I call, screeching at the parent; the bird swivels its head towards me and screeches back. None of that *hoot-hoot-who-who* nonsense; it's a territorial thing and there's a young'un sitting below it. I continue calling, on and off, for about fifteen minutes, until the bird becomes more aggressive, looking straight at me, and with one long, loud screech, announces—in no uncertain terms—that *this* is without question *its* territory. Right about then, I figure it's best to shut up, all the while hoping a small furry woodland creature would show up and give the owl something else to think about.

Standing in the river, I am alone; the only sounds are those of crickets, frogs, fishy splashes and the scoldings of a pair of belted kingfishers adding, "Yeah! Well! What *he* said goes for us, too, buddy," as they settle into a willow for the evening. This spot is secluded, and quite inaccessible. I can feel the cool evening air settling through my shirt, weighing heavily across my shoulders. Looking upriver, I can see marsh gas creeping from the dense vegetation of the left bank, spilling toward the center of the water. A creeping smudge, advancing slowly outward as the sun slips and the air temperature falls.

So, slip on your waders, feel the silence and come

out here beside me. Careful, there's a deep spot beside that big white boulder on your left ... that's it ... once you're onto this shoal you'll be fine. The water drops back down to just above your knees ... What did you say? ... Ho, those big splashes are carp, feeding on craneflies or the start of the daily *Hex* hatch ... the fish or the shad fly ... *Hexagenia limbata*, you know the big mayfly that's about an inch and a half long ... Ho, how big are the fish in here? ... Good question. Last year I got a 5-pound largemouth, the year before, a 4-pound smallmouth and someone caught an 18-pound pike in the spring ... What's that, the biggest carp? ... Hmmm, out of here, it's around 22 pounds ... On your 4-weight? ... Could be tricky ... Here, use my 6 ... there's 160 yards of backing on there ... just in case Old Yeller takes a daft turn, thinks outside the box again, inhaling this Spike off the surface ... Cast it over there, just to the edge of those shadows, in front of that big smooth rock ... That's it ... perfect ... now ... slowly ... very, very slowly ... twitch it ...

APPENDIX:
Fly Dressings

The Fly-tier

Dress me a fly in blue heron,
gold tinsel and teddy-bear eyes,
With the charm of precision-tied classics
when whirled through the harrowing skies.

Dusty Miller, Black Ranger, Blue Vulture,
seducing my equivocal mind.
I dream of symmetrical hair wings
and hackles like pink dandelions.

A fly with a cool personality,
compelling its leader to lure.
A fly that maintains its composure,
when wooed by a fish "connoisseur."

The wonder lies not in their spectrum,
nor winging or body techniques,
But the substance within their creator,
a gift that is truly unique.

Lisa A. Batt
January 22, 1985. Woodstock, Ontario

Art is the flower—Life is the green leaf.
Let every artist strive to make his flower a
beautiful living thing—something that will
convince the world that there may be—there
are—things more precious—more beautiful—
more lasting than life ...

Charles Rennie Mackintosh (1868–1928)

From the CD ROM:
Charles Rennie Mackintosh: Art, Architecture
   & Design
ISBN 0-9530838-0-2
© Wigwam Digital Ltd., 1997
Used with permission.

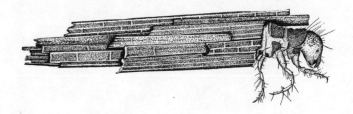

Fly choice—like the shade of a woman's lipstick, religion, your favorite sports team or the jacket design on a book cover—is a very personal thing. So, by no means am I trying to suggest you use these fly patterns. All I am saying is they work!

Some of the patterns are from the modern school of fly-tiers that includes Oliver Edwards, Jim McGeachie, Lloyd Keleher, Mart Klepp, Hans van Klinken, Gordon Michie, Paul Noble, Shane Reilly, Adam Sikora and some more from my own vise. Some are traditional, trustworthy patterns, developed over generations of angling use, which have proven to be productive. I have tried to get the history behind the pattern as close to the facts as I could. If I have omitted anything, the error is entirely mine, and I apologize in advance. Hey, drop me a line and let me know.

Fishing flies are not your best buddies, so do not get attached to them, and don't start crying if you snap one off. Working flies should be fished hard, but never put away wet, and with little—if any—regard or concern about their safety. If you are too afraid to drift a fly below a log jam for fear of busting off, I *guarantee* you will be missing fish. Stick to patterns that take minutes to make, and fish the hell out of them. You will be surprised at how many fish you will hook. I consider myself lucky if I get more than a dozen drifts from a fly without losing it. With this in mind, I never use head cement on my flies for several reasons: they never get the chance to unravel, I could tie a few more patterns instead of applying the cement, *and* I am convinced that since I can smell it so can the fish.

In these dressings I listed Mustad hook style numbers, because their worldwide popularity has made them readily available to the fly-tier. I am not endorsing these hooks, although 99 percent of my flies are tied on them.

Unless otherwise stated, the head and the tying thread are black.

Adams
Hook: 94840 sizes 12 to 16
Tail: Grizzly and brown hackle barbs mixed
Body: Gray fur dubbing, whatever you happen to have handy
Wing: A pair of grizzly hackle tips
Hackle: Grizzly and brown hackle

This is perhaps one of the most popular dry flies in use on the North American continent. It will catch trout, mooneyes and carp, and, when tied in a larger sizes, it is a useful smallmouth pattern, especially when it is tied in a parachute style.

Big Joe's Boatman
Hook: 3399 sizes 10 to 16
Tag: Two turns of pearl mylar tinsel, medium width, or, on the smaller sizes, a strand of pearl Krystal flash
Body: Cream embroidery wool D.M.C. #7905 (original), or #7579, which is a slightly darker color
Rib: Three or four turns of the tag material
Back: Brown plastic raffia
Oars: A "V" of webby hackle. Grouse or a speckled brown hen saddle feather
Head: Black ostrich herl (tied on after the back has been tied off)

I first began working on a Boatman fly in 1979, and I don't know how many changes the dressing has gone through to this final version. Attaching the "oars" is the trickiest part of tying the fly. After the ribbing has been tied off, the feather is nicked—the way you would a full-feather crayfish claw—and tied in at the head "good side down, eight or nine fibers on each side, with the curve sweeping up and toward the back." They are split and held in position when the shell back is drawn over and tied off. The only variation that I have seen is to use white plastic raffia for the back. When this change is made, a thin black line is drawn down the center of the body, along the top—why there, 'coz I don't think the fish can see it!—before ribbing the body and pulling over the shellback. Fly fishermen will often spend hours studying mayflies, stoneflies and caddis; however, they tend to skip over water boatmen as an important aquatic insect. Everybody knows what a corixa looks like, but few anglers fish them. It will work in rivers and in still water. I've used it for mooneye, bass, trout, crappies, sunfish, redhorse, drum and carp. This pattern has been my most productive fly for fishing quillback carp suckers. It is a very useful pattern when the water is clear. The fly is named after my father.

Big Joe's Crayfish

    Hook: 9671 sizes 4 to 12
    Feelers: A few fibers of male ringneck pheasant tail and one or two strands of pearl Krystal flash
    Claws: Dark speckled brown hen saddle, center removed to form a "V"
    Abdomen: Fluorescent red chenille
    Legs: Long natural red rooster
    Body: Beige chenille
    Back: Tan raffia
    Rib: Copper wire
    Tail: Surplus from the back, trimmed into a fan shape

This pattern developed at my vise in 1983 when I needed a realistic crayfish fly for fishing bass in clear water. It worked, and it has remained unchanged since I plucked the first one from my vise. The colors on this fly were used in developing the Outcast Crayfish. Without affecting its productivity, Paul Noble and I continually chopped bits off this pattern and used those results to concoct the much simpler fly. The pattern was named after my father. The original feathers used for the claws were the black and white body feathers from my jungle fowl skins.

Bitch Creek Nymph

Hook: 9672 sizes 6 to 10

Tail: Two strands of white rubber hackle

Body: Woven orange and black chenille

Thorax: Black chenille

Hackle: Natural red or brown rooster

Feelers: Same as the tail

Love it, or despise it, either way this pattern gets fish. It was developed in the States as a stonefly nymph for trout. However, it will catch a whack of carp, bass and pickerel, *if* you are willing to match the size of the fly to the water conditions. The Bitch Creek is usually heavily weighted and dragged along the riverbed.

Black Gnat

Hook: 3399 sizes 14 and 16

Body: Black floss

Wing: Starling quill

Hackle: Black hen

There are many variations on this traditional fly.

Most anglers fish the black gnat as a dry fly. The above is a wet-fly version that is believed to have been first tied by Mr. E. Todd, who developed it for fishing in the Scottish border areas. This is a great fly for taking trout up and down the length of Ontario.

Blue Thunder

Hook: 9671 sizes 2 to 12

Body: Flat silver tinsel

Rib: Oval silver tinsel

Wing: White calf tail

Topping: A few strands of purple Flashabou #6913

The Blue Thunder was my attempt at matching the popular salmon lure called the Cleo. On steelheading trips in the early 1980s, I was coming up short as my fishing buddies thumped fish. I duplicated the purple and silver of the Cleo, and started catching fish. I messed up when I named the fly, thinking the color of Flashabou was blue; it is most definitely purple. Over the years, the name has stuck, so there is little point in changing it now. The original dressing had a tail of golden pheasant crest and a body of embossed silver tinsel.

Booby

Hook: 9671 size 8
Tail: Tuft of black marabou
Body: Black seal's fur
Ribbing: Pearl Krystal flash
Eyes: Two egg-sack floaters in white spawn sacking

This fly was invented in England as a still-water trout fly. It was first tied by Gordon Fraser in the mid-1980s. Try to select big eyes for large hooks and smaller eyes for smaller hooks. Also try to ensure that the eyes are the same size. You wouldn't want the fly to swim lopsided or off-kilter, would you? Ethafoam can be used instead of the polystyrene floaters. It will last longer. The three most productive colors are black, white and purple. Although the Booby was designed as a rainbow fly, I've been using it for early spring carp or as a

surface pattern for summertime bass and crappies since about 1987. In 1994, Jay Kivell of Guelph began using a Chartreuse Booby as a surface pattern for gar pike.

The Buzby

Hook: 79580 sizes 6 and 8
Thread: Dark green size 6/0
Tail: Barred mallard flank
Body: Oval silver tinsel
Throat: A tuft of red marabou, hen fibers or wool
Underwing: A few strands of white bucktail
Midwing: Teal or mallard flank
Overwing: Gray squirrel tail dyed yellow

Originally tied as a bass fly in 1993 by Lloyd Keleher of Guelph, Ontario. Lloyd says, "I wanted a simple minnow type of pattern. It had to contain the most important bass-catching colors of red, silver and yellow. It is very eye-catching, and the bass mistake it for a small perch." In the summer this is a hard-to-beat smallmouth pattern. The Buzby is also a great pattern when the water has a good chop to it, and for fishing river mouths, especially when the steelhead are chasing minnows. Many anglers fish it using the upstream nymphing technique, which is rather unusual for this style of fly.

Cat's Whisker

>   Hook: 3399 sizes 6, 8 and 10
>   Body: Chartreuse medium-width chenille
>   Wing: White marabou
>   Eyes: A pair of silver bead chain

The Cat's Whisker was first tied in 1985 by David Train as a still-water rainbow trout fly for use in English reservoirs and ponds. It is a good pattern for steelhead, brown trout, salmon, mooneye, gar pike and carp. It works, especially when the water is very cold or off-colored. An all-black version of this pattern is a highly productive dressing for fishing at night. It is well worth having a few of these in your box. It is best to fish this pattern on a floating line without a dropper. David Train's original fly had a tail of white marabou and a ribbing of flat silver tinsel. These can be omitted from the fly without affecting its productivity.

Claret Dabbler

>   Hook: 3399 sizes 6 to 12
>   Tail: Three male ringneck pheasant fibers, tied long
>   Body: Claret seal's fur
>   Rib: Gold wire
>   Hackle: Natural red rooster
>   Collar: Bronze mallard, tied long

This is an Irish pattern originating in the Dromore Angling Club in Bandbridge, County Down, in the late 1980s for use on Lough Melvin and Lough Erne. Its creation is attributed to Donald McClaren. If you're going to fish in the brown-trout loughs of Western Ireland, you will have one of these on your cast. The Dabbler is designed to be pulled through the water just under the surface. It is usually the middle fly on a three-fly cast, fishing loch-style. In Ontario, it will catch speckles, splake, browns and rainbows. It can be fished in rivers or in the Great Lakes. I've used it fishing loch-style to catch steelhead in Georgian Bay, lower Lake Huron and Lake Erie. In Lake Ontario it will also catch salmon, which is a bit on the scary side, using fly gear. I've been using it as a handy-dandy smallmouth pattern, fished just below the surface, since the mid-1980s. Basil Shields has been instrumental in expanding the range of this pattern, down as far as Tasmania, where the fly is catching on like bunnies have in Australia.

Cranefly

    Hook: 94840 sizes 8 to 14
    Body: Male ringneck pheasant tail fibers
    Thorax: Peacock herl
    Legs: Six, single-knotted pheasant-tail fibers
    Wings: A pair of furnace, cree or badger Indian rooster hackle tips
    Hackle: Same as the wings, tied sweeping back to the hook point

There are hundreds of adult Cranefly patterns; this one happens to be the one I use the most. I've been fishing with it since 1982 and it has proven to be very effective in both still water and rivers. Fly fishermen on this side of the Atlantic are just starting to wake up to the fish-catching potential of a surface Cranefly. It will take carp, bass, steelhead, crappies, speckles, browns, sheephead, pickerel and, on occasion, whitefish. If you are fishing the fly in still water for steelhead or smallmouth, do not twitch it. Grease it up, chuck it out and let the fish find the fly. When they do, I'd like to take this opportunity to wish you the "best of luck," as you are probably going to need it.

Crunchy Caddis

    Hook: 3399 sizes 6 to 14 or 9671 sizes 8 to 16
    Body: Any kind of gray-fur dubbing wrapped thickish
    Case: Palmered natural red rooster clipped and trimmed "spiky" to the width of the hook gap

Thorax: Two turns of yellow wool or dubbing
Legs: A turn of speckled hen, grouse or dark partridge
Head: Black ostrich herl

This pattern developed at my vise in 1988. Bob Church had just published his book *Bob Church's Guide to Trout Flies* (ISBN 0-94628-449-0) and I thought that the Cave's Caddis Larva, with its peeking-out thorax, listed in the book, was going to be a cracker of a trout and steelhead fly. It was, but it took too long to make—too much blending. I had been having great success with a clipped hackle fly, the Wonder Nymph, taken from Mike Dawes' 1986 book, *The Flytier's Manual* (ISBN 0-088317-130-9). I combined what I thought were the "good bits" from these two patterns and added the black ostrich herl head from my Big Joe's Boatman. All I am willing to say is, "it catches oodles of fish, all year long." It will work on steelhead, browns, bass, carp, redhorse, sheephead, crappies, salmon, channel catfish, speckles, whitefish, grayling, white and hog suckers and, in very small sizes, gizzard shad. The fly gets its name from the finished pattern, having a decidedly "crunchy" look to it. The trick to making Crunchy Caddises quickly is to trim the rooster feather *before* you tie it in. Prepare a bag of these in advance when you are watching hockey or football on T.V. The thorax is applied after the hackle has been palmered and tied off, then the legs are added—don't go heavy on these—then the head.

Dexter

Hook: 9671 sizes 2 to 16
Body: Flat silver tinsel
Rib: Oval silver tinsel
Wing: White calf tail
Topping: A few strands of red Flashabou #6911

I invented this pattern in the early 1980s, when I needed a copy of the Mepps Red and White #3 lure. My fishing buddies were catching large amounts of smallmouth bass on this red, white and silver lure, while I washed flies. The original items used on the fly wing were red calf tail, or red Christmas-tree tinsel. In 1982 I began using red Flashabou in the dressing, and it has never changed. The Dexter is a good smallmouth and largemouth bass pattern. It will also take steelhead and salmon, especially when the water is low. In a size 2 or larger, it will take pike and muskie. Unlike many other pike and muskie patterns, the small size of the fly allows it to be fished on light tackle. If you have never landed a pike on a 4-weight, I strongly suggest you give it a try.

Double Elk Hair Caddis

Hook: 94840 size 8

Tag: A turn or two of pearl mylar

Tail: A stubby clump of pearl Krystal flash

Body: White rabbit, dubbed thick and scuffed up

Rib: A strip of stretched pearl mylar

Wing: Two bunches of elk or coastal deer, the tips all lining up just past the bend

I invented this in the fall of 1981 as a bushy rainbow fly for fast broken water. Looking at it in my vise, it screamed, "I'm gonna catch oodles." Watching it drifting along like a beachball, through a set of rapids, gave me the feeling of "Any time now!" It was a remarkable failure. For two years I fished it with hardly a swirl. On a smallmouth-bass trip in 1982, I tried it at the seam of a fast eddy. Three casts and three fish. Being quick off the mark, I made a mental note to try it in different colors. As a bass fly, it is best fished on the surface of slow pools. Chuck it out and don't twitch it or move it. Leave it alone and make sure that it drifts without disturbing the water surface. Other good colors are gray and black. The wing is always the natural hair color. By fishing it over the years, I have been very successful using it as a spring steelhead pattern, especially on sunny days and in slow water.

For fun I tied up Jim McGeachies' Halloween Caddis using this two-wing style and it has produced some very large bass and salmon. The first wing should be inserted in the center of the golden-olive seal's fur. The best sizes are 6 and 8.

The dressing for the Halloween Caddis follows on p. 183.

Dunkeld Dabbler

    Hook: 3399 sizes 6 to 12
      Tail: Golden pheasant crest and three long male ringneck pheasant fibers.
     Body: Flat gold tinsel
      Rib: Gold wire
  Hackle: Orange rooster, palmered
  Collar: Bronze mallard, tied long

This fly took the largest fish of the 1995 Commonwealth Fly Fishing Championships on Loch Leven, Scotland. It is a mix of the traditional Scottish pattern the Dunkeld, and the Irish pattern the Dabbler. Tom Murray and I had been using Dabblers in practice, and under difficult conditions we had a few fish strike or follow. Gordon Michie, one of Scotland's top professional tiers and an ex-captain of their World Fly Fishing team, gave the Canadians some advice on fishing Loch Leven: "Whatever you do, keep a Dunkeld on your cast."

Gordon lives in the town of Ballingry, about a ten-minute drive from Loch Leven, so his advice was taken to heart. I altered the traditional wet-fly style of the Dunkeld and tied it in the Irish style. The last day of practice produced eighteen fish for Tom and me, one of which was around 6 pounds. On the first morning of the competition—on a fly tied in the Green Hotel in Kinross, two hours before the start of the event—under flat, calm conditions, with bright sunlight, Tom hooked and landed the big fish. I had one in the boat at 49 cm, but out of the corner of my eye I was watching Tom play an obviously larger fish. After he landed it, we drifted over to his boat and, with a large grin, he flashed a 55-cm sign. I felt like banging my head on the gunwale. The pattern works when it is stripped, or on the hang after retrieving a cast. In Georgian Bay and Lake Ontario, it will work fishing traditional loch-style as a point, or dropper, fly. In rivers, it will take steelhead, browns, bass, salmon and speckled trout. It fishes best under clear, bright conditions. As a point of interest, Loch Leven is one of the original sources for the stocking of brown trout into North America—Germany was the other—and for a time Mary Queen of Scots was imprisoned in Loch Leven Castle, on one of two islands in the middle of the loch.

Feeble Freestone

    Hook: 3399 sizes 6 to 16

      Tail: A few strands of pearl Krystal flash and grizzly hen fibers

      Rib: Pearl Krystal flash

    Body: White seal's fur dubbing

    Thorax: Same as the body with a touch of pink mixed in. Well picked-out

    Wingcase: Pearl Krystal flash. This is pulled down to form the throat

    Throat: Pearl Krystal flash

    Collar: Grizzly hen fibers, tied in front of the collar

    Head: Tan or gray thread

I began devising white nymphs in Scotland for grayling. They worked, but were spectacularly unproductive on many occasions. When I crossed the Atlantic in 1979, I still found the fly lacking. I added the pink thorax to my original white nymphs and found it to be very productive for steelhead, browns and resident rainbows. This no-name pattern—without Krystal flash—has become popular with float fishermen and fly fishermen on many Southern Ontario rivers. After Paul introduced the Freestone Nymph in 1989, I knew he was onto something, so I added the Krystal flash to my earlier efforts. The result was amazing. Since the Feeble Freestone was born in the fall of 1990, it has never been modified. It is a very productive fly for steelhead and salmon in the Georgian Bay area and in the Credit, Bronte and Ganaraska river systems. John Liberatore of Guelph took four fish—2, 4, 7 and 10 pounds—in ten casts from the Collingwood area, steelheading in 1994. The Feeble Freestone will work in clear or slightly off-color water. It is a good fly to use when fishing in a rainstorm. I've yet to figure out why.

Freestone Nymph

Hook: 3399 sizes 6 to 12; 9671 sizes 8 to 14
Tail: A few strands of pearl Krystal flash and black hen hackle barbs
Body: Black seal's fur or substitute
Rib: Pearl Krystal flash
Thorax: Same as the body. Well picked-out
Wingcase: Pearl Krystal flash. This is pulled down to form the throat
Throat: Pearl Krystal flash
Collar: Black hen hackle, tied in front of the throat

First tied by Paul Noble of London, Ontario, in 1989. This is a "must have" nymph for any of the freestone steelhead rivers. The Krystal flash represents bubbles, so a little goes a long way. It is now one of the most productive steelhead nymphs in the province, bar none. Paul "knows no fear" when designing flies. He has no regard for tradition, conformations or the purity of a pattern, and will throw caution to the wind if he believes what he is working on will at some point produce fish.

His results can be horrid-looking, but they do tend to take fish. The Freestone Nymph was his first foray into designing a fly, and he got it spot on. It will also take bass, salmon, pickerel, carp, mooneye, redhorse, browns and drum.

Fuzzy Wuzzy

Hook: 9671 sizes 2 to 14
Tail: Black squirrel
Body: Black chenille or wool
Hackle: Two black rooster feathers tied in by the tip. One is tied in halfway along the body. A larger one is tied in at the head

At the time of writing this, I know of only one other angler in Ontario who fishes this New Zealand pattern, and he wishes to remain nameless as he is known as a dry-fly fisherman. Hey, as long as I keep getting those used unmarked bills in the brown envelopes, I'm willing to keep it hush-hush. This sleeper of a fly has been completely passed over by the fly-fishing community. It was invented in the 1930s by Fred Fletcher, the owner of Waita-hanui Lodge in New Zealand. He developed the fly as an imitation of a crayfish for use in night fishing. The hackle represents the legs of the *koura,* or cray-fish. When it is pulled through the water in short tugs, the legs pulsate, giving the fly life. Small-mouth bass love this fly, as do rainbows, browns and salmon. It will work from dusk to dawn in lakes, ponds or rivers. It is a highly productive steelhead pattern, especially when fishing river mouths in low light. I've had good success using it through the day for carp. It can be tied with a red body, which is a better color to use at the back end of bass season.

Golden-Olive Bumble

Hook: 3906 or 3399 sizes 8 to 12
Tail: Golden pheasant crest
Body: Golden-olive seal's fur
Rib: Gold wire or fine oval gold tinsel
Hackle: Golden-olive and natural red rooster palmered together along the body
Collar: Blue jay

This is a very, very popular loch-style fly, invented by Mr. Justice Theodore Kingsmill Moore. If you ever get the chance to fish on any of the great still-water fisheries of Britain, you will at some point have a Golden-Olive Bumble on your cast. I've been using it since 1983 in Ontario and it has produced some savage hits—and some very fine rainbows—from Lake Ontario, Georgian Bay and Lake Erie.

In rivers or lakes, this fly will catch smallmouth bass, pickerel, speckles, steelhead, splake, rockbass and crappies. According to Basil Shields, one of Ireland's best gillies and fly tiers, if you substitute the blue jay with dyed guinea hen, you will be "wasting your time fishing the fly." He is right, this time around; a feather substitution will not work. In fishing a Bumble make sure that it is just below the water and, when retrieved, produces a bump in the surface. It is usually fished as the bob fly. Partner it with a Claret Dabbler—in any posi-tion of a three-fly cast—and wonderful things happen. *Irish Trout and Salmon Flies* by E.J. Malone (ISBN 0-86140-180-8) is a great source for more information on Bumbles, Murroughs and the like.

Gravel Bed

    Hook: 3399 sizes 12 to 16

    Body: Peacock sword fiber stripped of flue

    Thorax: A few turns of purple tying thread or
        purple floss

    Wing: Matching slips of hen ringneck
        pheasant tail, without the black
        markings

    Hackle: Long black rooster, tied very sparse

The gravel-bed insect looks like a small cranefly (*Hexatoma fuscipennis,* according to John Roberts). It is not aquatic, living in the sand and gravel, close to the water's edge—hence the name. Although this pattern is a very old one from the U.K., it catches oodles of trout in North America and, in larger sizes, bass. It is well worth having a few of these in your box.

Green Peter

    Hook: 3399 sizes 8 to 14

    Body: Light green seal's fur

    Rib: Fine gold wire

    Hackle: Red rooster

    Wing: Center tail fibers from a female ring-
        neck pheasant. If you have difficulty
        working with these, use matching
        quill slips from the wing of the bird

I was introduced to this Irish wet fly by David Hall, one of the top guides on Lough Mask, when I was fishing at the World Championships in 1995. Since then I've used it in trout rivers and lakes across Canada, and found that, all season long, it produced fish, especially in the smaller sizes. A size 8 is useful for summertime bass, if fished deep. Like the Bumbles and the Dabblers this will produce fish in the Great Lakes when fished loch-style. John Roberts lists the Green Peter as a copy of the caddis fly *Phryganea varia*, which hatches in the middle of the Irish summertime.

Halloween Caddis

    Hook: Your favourite steelhead dry fly with
        sizes to match the water conditions

    Tail: Gray speckled partridge

Butt: Orange-red seal's fur
Body: 3/4 dubbed golden-olive seal fur
 1/4 dubbed red antron,
 well picked out to form a throat
Rib: Oval gold tinsel
Wing: Deer body, dyed a reddish-brown
Head: The butt ends of the wing trimmed
 and lacquered
Thread: Orange

Jim McGeachie—a talented tier and a skilled and successful guide—took almost four years to create this pattern. His hard work paid off in 1987, and he has given steelhead fishermen a hell of a surface pattern. This fly catches fish. Lots of fish. Although a resident of Innerkip, Ontario, Jim developed this fly for fishing the fall runs in upper Michigan where he guides. This pattern is a "must have" when fall fishing and works best in fast broken water and tailouts. The fly is also a good surface pattern for summer smallmouth, especially when the water is very low or clear. I have found the best sizes to be a 10 or 12, 36890, for steelhead or a size 8 or 10, 94840, for smallmouth and gar pike. The 94840, tied in sizes 12 to 16, is a handy-dandy brown trout and grayling fly.

Klepps Killer
Hook: 9671 sizes 14 and 16
 Tail: A tuft of black marabou
 Body: Peacock herl

This fly was invented by Mart Klepp of Guelph in 1984. It was designed as a spring carp fly for fishing in Guelph Lake. Mart and I had been fishing carp in March, just after the ice had moved out. The water was crystal clear, and the fish spooky and sluggish. We needed a pattern that would sink slowly, have lots of movement and not be gaudy enough to give the fish coronaries when they saw it. Mart, a brilliant and methodical creator of flies, went home and came up with this little gem. The following day we fished it in a snow squall and managed to produce two carp each. It is best fished without a dropper on a long leader of about 4-pound test. It has also produced mooneye, bass, crappies, perch, speckles, splake and steelhead. In the summer it can be tied on a #6 hook and it will work on larger carp.

Klinkhamer Special

Hook: Partridge K12ST or GRS12ST sizes 8 to 16

Body: Light tan to brown synthetic dubbing; Fly Rite Extra Fine Poly #'s 19, 20, 32 and 39

Wing: White poly yarn (pink for low light or fast riffles)

Thorax: Bronze peacock herl

Hackle: (Parachute) blue dun, chestnut, grizzly or cree

If you like to fish dry flies—I know some of you do and I have heard rumors that this is catching on—you *must, must, must* have some of these hatching caddis patterns in your fly box. End of story. This is an amazing fly with an amazing success rate. It might just be the best surface searching pattern in the known universe. Dutchman Hans van Klinken created it in 1985 on a fishing trip to Norway, and the fly-fishing community owes him a huge thanks. This is the fly John Roberts used on the Grand River near Fergus to hook eight brown trout in eight casts. I have never been a fan of dry flies, but this performance convinced me that *this one* was a brilliant pattern and one worth tying up. Since then, I have sung its praises at many public speaking engagements, filled orders for thousands of them, and over the years I have accumulated a mitt-ful of letters from those who have tried it and taken lots of fish on it. An important part of constructing the fly is putting a slight bend in the shank about a quarter of the way back from the eye. The thorax is dressed over this flat section and this is critical in making the fly sit flush on the water surface. Full tying instructions can be found in Oliver Edwards' book *Flytyers Masterclass*. The fly will catch salmon, grayling, speckles, browns, steelhead, smallmouth bass, carp, mooneye, splake, whitefish, gar and pickerel. Thank you Hans van Klinken.

Kolking's Caddis

> Hook: 94840 sizes 14 to 18
> Body: Male ringneck pheasant tail fibers,
> well marked, from mature birds
> Wing: Natural-colored elk hock or coastal
> deer
> Horns: A pair of male ringneck fibers

I tied this in 1979 as a dry fly for browns and specks. I was catching lots of fish on Payne Collier's dry-fly pheasant tail, a pattern I'd brought over from the old country. At the time it was nearly impossible to get honey dunn feathers for the tail and hackle, and Al Troth's Elk Hair Caddis was becoming popular. I found I could get just as many fish on his pattern when I omitted the hackle. So I didn't bother to add one to the caddis I'd created. All I did was to wrap the pheasant feathers for the body, and stick a bunch of elk hair on top for the wing. Simple enough to do and very productive. I added the feelers that winter when I was looking to construct a series of realistic patterns, just for the fun of doing it. In 1981 on the Bayfield River I used them to catch rainbow. I'm not sure if the antenna make the fly more productive when fishing, but they do make the flies look very cute and realistic when they are in the box. Tied without the antenna, it is called a Toots Caddis, which has taken more than its fair share of fish from the Grand River. Both the Kolkings and the Toots patterns were originally called pheasant tail caddis. The fly is named after Andrea Kolking, who after seeing the flies lined up in one of my boxes, was taken aback by their realism and decided to try fly fishing. On her first trip out, she landed a 5-pound pike on a Dexter, using a 4-weight rod. "Ya gotta like it!"

Loch Ness Lemming

> Hook: Three, size 2 or 4, 3399 or 3366
> Tail: A strip of gray muskrat
> Body: Three sections, gray muskrat strips
> wrapped around the hook shanks.
> Held together by two loops of wire
> or 40-pound mono
> Eyes: (optional) A pair of nickel
> bead chain

Whiskers: (optional) Two bunches of
moose mane

Paul Noble of London says, "This fly was invented in 1990 as an uglier version of the Plonker (see p. 192). It was designed to get the fish's attention." It will catch pike, bowfin and muskie. This fly is not for use by the faint of heart as it can produce some savage strikes. The mobile materials used in its construction mean that little manipulation of the line is required to produce hits. The slower the fly is fished the more effective it will be. Trolling it behind a full sinking line is a useful technique for fishing river mouths in the fall. Using a floating line in the spring, this is a good pike and muskie pattern, especially around weed beds or post-spawning areas.

Mackerel Nymph

Hook: 3399 sizes 8 to 14 (original
Tiemco 2457)
Body: Olive green dubbing
Thorax: Black wool
Rib: Clear mono
Back: A strip of smoked-mackerel skin

This caddis-nymph imitation was devised by the Polish nymph fisherman Adam Sikora. Have a peek under a few rocks in any river—lift them out of the water first—and you will see "bugs" that look remarkably like this fly. They look like little green maggots. The mackerel nymph should be in everyone's box. It is a great searching fly, and it has produced countless fish for me, often in very difficult conditions. It will catch brown trout, speckles and steelhead all across Canada, and has also taken crappies, bass, whitefish, mooneye, suckers and panfish. You can switch the body to wool and the thorax to dubbing without affecting the fish-catching properties of the fly. If you're out of smoked-mackerel skin, use a section of brown plastic raffia for the back. My father, although not a fly fisherman, produced an interesting innovation by switching the body to cream embroidery wool, D.M.C. #7171, but retaining the black-dubbed thorax. To make the pattern more appealing, especially for steelhead, add a strip of mylar tinsel under the back. Use gold tinsel on the green body but silver on the cream-colored wool. You'll hardly notice the change when the fly is in the vise, but you will when it is wet. The tinsel bleeds through the back, making the fly very "yummy" and lifelike. I introduced the tinsel to the pattern on a steelhead trip in the fall 1993, the same year that noted British angling author John Roberts introduced me to this pattern, and to Hans van Klinkens' Klinkhamer Special, on a fishing trip to the Grand River near Fergus, Ontario. Using a Klinkhamer, he rose eight fish in eight casts in a riffle that had just been "fished hard" by a group of very loud anglers. John was the first person in the province to catch a fish on these patterns and, arguably, in Canada. His book, *Collins Illustrated Dictionary of Trout Flies* (ISBN 0-00-218491-5), is invaluable, and should be on every fly-tier's shelf.

Murray

Hook:	Partridge, Bartleet CS10 traditional, size 1/0
Tag:	Flat silver tinsel
Butt:	Black ostrich herl
Tail:	Strands of peacock sword feather
Ribbing:	French oval silver tinsel size 15
Body:	(rear half) Purple floss
	(mid section) Embossed silver tinsel
	(front half) Black seal's fur dubbing
Hackle:	Ringneck pheasant rump dyed purple
Collar:	Speckled guinea fowl feather
Wing:	2 pairs of rooster feathers dyed red 2 pairs of ringneck pheasant dyed purple
Cheek:	Strands of peacock sword feather

This is the dressing for the fly on the cover of the book. It is a full-feather wing version of the steelhead pattern created by the late Murray Barrett and myself on a 1991 trip to the Bruce Peninsula in Ontario. In high water he had been hooking fish on purple patterns and I on black flies, so we combined these colors into one fly. Bingo! The fishing version of the fly we created is a follows:

Hook: 36890 sizes 2 to 10
Tag: Flat silver tinsel
Tail: Purple hen fibers
Rib: Oval silver tinsel
Body: (rear half) Purple wool
      (front half) Black wool or seal's fur
Wing: Gray squirrel tail dyed purple
Hackle: Purple fronted by guinea hen

The original pattern had an underwing of red calf tail, but we dropped this without damaging the fish-catching properties of the fly. (One less thing to tie in.) This fly has been successful on steelhead, brown trout, splake, smallmouth bass and salmon. My clients have used it to take steelhead in Argentina, Atlantic salmon in both Scotland and Norway, and sea trout in Ireland. Please note that there is an older Scottish salmon fly—which has fallen out of popularity—called a Murray. It was often dressed on very large hooks and had the distinction of having two wings (one tied halfway along the body and the other at the head) in order for the finished wing to reach from the eye to the bend.

Murrough
Hook: 94840 sizes 6 or 8
Body: Claret seal's fur
Rib: Fine gold wire
Hackle: Two natural red rooster feathers, palmered together along the body
Wing: Dark speckled turkey
Horns: Two well marked male pheasant tail fibres extending an inch over the eye

This is a dry version of a large red Irish caddis, which hatches during the last of the summer. There is no way to describe this pattern, other than ugly, but, boy, can it catch fish. To make the wing, cut a wide strip of fibers, then fold it over so that it is doubled. It is then tied in like a traditional wet-fly wing, so it takes on a tent shape.

Cut the wing square, about a half an inch longer than the body. This fly is very productive for steelhead, browns and smallmouth bass, especially in the fall. It will work in rivers and in lakes, where the takes are unmistakable and often spectacular.

Orange Mugwump
Hook: 9671 sizes 2 to 6
Tail: A tuft of the body material, if you feel like tying it in
Body: Burnt orange D.M.C. embroidery wool #7436 or golden-orange #7505
Rib: Clear 8-pound mono and flat gold tinsel
Wing: A light gray zonker strip of mink
Fins: A pair of light partridge feathers, flared outward
Head: Olive or brown sculpen wool
Eyes: A pair of silver nickel bead chain

This fly came into being in a rather roundabout way. I'm a big fan of muddlers and sculpins. I fish them for steelhead, bass, pickerel, pike, muskie, splake, sheephead, speckles, bowfin, salmon and crappies. Quite often one of North America's most elusive game fish, the carp, will take sculpins or muddlers fished deep. The first fly rolled off my tying bench in 1989, as just another carping fly. It was originally known as an Orange Sculpin, no lack of creativity there, and fished as a baby perch imitation. It was renamed in 1993 by one of my fishing buddies, "Dry Fly" David, after he read *Naked Lunch.* It is best fished on a long leader, 15 feet of 6-pound mono, with a small split shot 4 inches up from the fly. Try fishing it using an upstream nymphing technique on a shorter leader. The original pattern had a head made from natural dark-brown wool rovings. This was changed when sculpen wool became more readily available in Canada. A useful variation of this pattern, called a Penguin, is tied as follows:

Hook: 9671 sizes 2 to 6
Tail: A tuft of the body wool and a few strands of pearl Krystal flash
Body: White D.M.C. embroidery wool

Rib: Clear 8-pound mono and flat
  silver tinsel
Wing: A strip of black rabbit
Fins: A pair of black hen saddle feathers
Head: Black sculpen wool
Eyes: A pair of silver nickel bead chain

The Penguin is a great steelhead and pike fly, especially when the water is very cold and clear. It is also a cracker of a pattern for backend bass. It was named by Willie "The Kid" McLennan, "Coz it looks like a penguin."

Shane Reilly, an innovative tier and fisherman from the Winters Hatches Fly Fishing Club in Toronto, replaced the fur strip with three sections—one at the tail, one at the midpoint on the body and one behind the head—of damsel green marabou. On both the Mugwump and the Penguin, this change in the wing produces a better pattern for use in slow pools.

Outcast Crayfish
  Hook: 9671 sizes 4 to 14
  Claws: Two chunks of olive rabbit
  Body: Medium-width beige or tan chenille
Ribbing: Copper wire
  Back: Tan plastic raffia, trimmed to form
    a tail

This fly was a team effort by Paul Noble and me. It rose from the scraps from our tying benches—the cast-off items heading for the garbage can—hence the name. This pattern is easy to tie, and in the fall a heck of a bass pattern. The small size and mobile claws make it irresistible to bass, carp, steelhead, drum, rockbass, redhorse and browns. From August to November, smaller crayfish patterns produce more fish than the larger summer sizes.

Peter Ross
  Hook: 3399 sizes 8 to 16
  Tail: Golden pheasant crest
  Body: Back half, flat silver tinsel; front half
    red seal's fur

Rib: Fine silver wire or oval silver tinsel
Hackle: Black rooster or hen, whatever you
have handy
Wing: Well-marked teal flank

This is perhaps one of the most underused fish-catching, small-minnow patterns in Canada. It will catch browns, salmon, steelhead and speckles. It was designed by Peter Ross (1873–1923), the owner of a small shop in Killin, a town nestled at the southern tip of Loch Tay and the River Dochart. Ross didn't tie flies, and he had a local tier produce this version of the Teal and Red. When I was a kid, I fished a Peter Ross with a bright orange hackle. This variation was "locally popular"—rumor had it that this change originated in Gourock or Greenock along the Firth of Clyde—and it took a lot of fish. I've used this version, and the original, for steelhead, brown trout, salmon, smallmouth and crappies, having had great success with them on bright sunny days. The orange should be "clear and crisp," with a good sheen to it, not dull or washed out. The rest is history.

Plonker
Hook: Size 2, 3399 or 3366
Tail: Strip of muskrat fur
Body: Muskrat fur strip, cut across the
grain and wrapped along the shank
Eyes: A pair of nickel bead chain

This is an easy fly to tie. It came into being in the summer of 1984. I had been using some strymph-like flies for bass but started picking up a few pike and pickerel. I was using a dubbing loop method for spinning up the bodies, but it took far too long to cover the hook shank using this technique. Then, when I scuffed them up with a BBQ scraper or Velcro, much of the fur came out. A year or two earlier I had tied some "bunny" type patterns for a client who was heading to Alaska. In creating the Plonker, I used the bunny technique but with a natural-colored fur. I made about a dozen, then I couldn't resist adding the tail and the eyes. On its first outing to Sarnia it produced a carp of 20 pounds, a few pike and a pickerel. If you're going to fish pike in the shallows, keep the chain off the fly for a slower drop through the water column. The Plonker is an awfully good smallmouth pattern. The fly's name is derived from two sources. The first is the "plonk" sound it makes when it hits the water. The second is from a favorite affectionate Scottish saying from my father. When he first saw the flies, he said, "Yir no gonna use them, are ye? They're plonkers." He was right.

The Post-OviPosting Adult (POPA) Caddis

Hook: Partridge Grub K4A sizes 8 to 18
Body: Olive or brown synthetic dubbing
Thorax: Natural deer hair, chopped and spun
Rib: Fine gold wire on the body only
Gills: Ostrich herl the same color as the body
Wing: Brown plastic raffia, trimmed to shape
Head: Thread to match the body color

It's harder to pronounce the name of this fly than it is to tie it. This pattern is from the bench of Oliver Edwards. In some species of caddis, the adult females swim underwater to deposit their eggs. They will swim down to the riverbed and stick their eggs to anything that's solid. When this is done, they will drift back up to the surface, and, for want of a better term, "rehatch." The key here is that they don't swim back up to the water surface, they *drift* up, making them easy targets for hungry fish. This is a great fly for catching browns, rainbows, speckles and smallmouth bass. It can be tied with a set of antennae made from moose mane. If you're trout fishing and you don't have these in your box, you might as well be sitting at home watching paint dry or TV reruns. Full tying instructions for this pattern can be found in the book *Oliver Edwards' Flytyers Masterclass* (ISBN 0-88317-179-1).

Rusty Rat

Hook: 36890 sizes 4 to 10
Tag: Oval gold tinsel
Tail: Peacock swords
Body: Back half, yellow floss; front half, peacock herl

Veiling: Strands of the body floss
 Rib: Oval gold tinsel
Hackle: Grizzly
 Wing: Gray fox fur
 Head: Red thread

This is perhaps one of the most famous Atlantic salmon patterns in existence. It will also catch steelhead and bass. There is a bit of a debate as to who invented this pattern: most say it was J. Clovis Asenault in Atholville, New Brunswick, as a copy of an unraveling Black Rat that was showing its rusty underbody of dental floss. Others give credit to Dr. O. Summers of New Jersey.

Scud
 Hook: 3399 sizes 10 to 16
 Body: Hare's ear or hare's mask
 Rib: Clear mono
 Back: A thin strip of clear plastic
  Ziploc bag
 Head: Brown or gray thread

There are hundreds of scud patterns. This one is easy to tie and it catches fish. It works 365 days a year, and it will catch rainbows, speckles, browns, panfish, carp and redhorse. Scuff the body up with a chunk of Velcro to "make it stick out like legs." Don't be afraid to use scud patterns when it's minus 10, 2 feet of snow blanket the bank, and you're fishing winter steelhead. Some tiers incorporate a section of bright orange or red dubbing in the center of the body. This imitates a parasitic infection often seen in scuds, making the fly more visible to the fish.

Smushed Hopper
 Hook: 9671 sizes 4 to 10
 Tail: A loop of yellow tapestry wool
 Body: Yellow tapestry wool
 Wing: A thick bunch of male ringneck
  tail fibers
Hackle: Grouse
 Head: Golden-olive or dark-olive deer hair
  (Veniards golden olive)

There are lots of grasshopper patterns available, so why should you use this one? Two reasons: It works and it is very easy to tie. Most hoppers are designed to be fished on the surface; however, this one works best when dragged along the bottom and fished deep. It has to be quick to construct so that when you get "snagged up and busted off," it's no big deal. I've used it for browns, speckles, bass and carp. If you can catch the first run of fall salmon or steelhead, it will take fish. This is a great smallmouth pattern that will work from the season opener to closing. I've been using it since the first one crawled out of my vise in the early 1980s. The fly was named by Willie McLennan, his brother Ben and sister Lauren, who all agreed that, when wet, the fly looked like a "smushed-up grasshopper." Some tiers use sculpen wool for the head, but I've found that spun deer hair works better. Perhaps the deer hair moves more erratically when it is being fished, who knows? Some anglers use various types of loop knots to attach the fly to their leader. This type of connection will make the fly more mobile in the water. It's quite alarming just how many fish this fly will take.

Spike

    Hook: 3366 size 2
    Body: Spun and clipped natural
        deer hair
    Hackle: One or two natural red or black
        rooster palmered
    Legs: 4 white rubber legs (6 if you feel like
        the extra work)

This spun-and-clipped deer-hair pattern was developed at my vise in 1983 as a surface fly for smallmouth bass. The original had legs made from the replacement skirts of bass lures, then I switched to living rubber. However, since Mark Rippen of Guelph introduced me to the fine art of stripping apart old bungie cords, I've never looked back. The rubber in these cords seems "softer" with more kick to them—thus more action—than anything else I have tried. The fly *has* to ride half on the surface, so *do not* pack the hair as tightly as you would on an Atlantic salmon Bomber. Plus, by keeping the hair loose, the fish will hang onto it and take a few extra chomps before they spit it out. Tie the hackle in by the tip and work it into the hair as you palmer it. These flies take an awful beating when you fish them, so you want to try to protect the hackle as best you can. The hackle should be quite long, making this a great opportunity to use up all those big feathers at the base of your capes. *Do not* use a high-grade hackle or the fly will ride too high on the water surface. The Spike has taken hundreds of smallmouth for me, a few salmon and a bunch of steelhead. It is also a useful pickerel pattern, especially when the lower half of the body has been colored black with a marker. If you feel guilty about not matching the hatch, chop off the legs and convince yourself you are fishing a cicada bug! You'll get more fish by giving it slow twitches, or none at all, than you will by moving it fast enough to give yourself a nose bleed. Other good colors are entirely—hair, legs and hackle—purple, black or olive.

Spring's Wiggler

Hook: 3399 sizes 6 to 12, or 9671 sizes 8 to 12

Tail: Red squirrel or fox squirrel tail tips

Body: Fluorescent red chenille

Back: Butts from the tail pulled over

Hackle: Palmered natural red or black rooster

Rib: (optional) A counter wrap of clear mono

This is one variation of the hundreds of color combinations for this fly. In their book *Flies for Steelhead* (ISBN 0-936644-08-7), Dick Stewart and Farrow Allen give an accurate account of the history of the pattern, listing it as Spring's Wiggler, invented in the 1960s by Ron and Frank Spring of Muskegon, Michigan. This pattern is effective on steelhead, salmon, brown trout, crappies and bass.

Torpedo

Hook: 9671 sizes 6 and 8

Tail: Marabou

Hackle: Two or three turns of black or natural red rooster

Head: Brass or black bead, fronted by a built-up, tapered head of thread the same color as the tail

This pattern was developed by the folk at the Townhill Angling Club in Dunfermline, Scotland, in 1993. It was first shown to me in 1997 by Gordon Michie on a trip to Loch Leven. Due to high winds, the loch was unfishable, and Gordon and I sat in his car, exchanging fly patterns. This fly was developed for fishing rainbow and brown trout, and it does a hell of a job. It is also a great fly for bass, pickerel, carp, drum and speckles. Once you start using this pattern, it is difficult to switch to something else. The best colors for the tail seem to be black, orange and olive. For steelhead, try purple or that eyeball-offensive, bubblegum-pink color.

Wee Muddler

Hook: 94840 sizes 18 and 20

Tail: Speckled hen fibers or dark grouse

Body: Flat gold mylar

Wing: Same as the tail

Head: Spun and clipped caribou

I tied this in 1985 as a bit of a joke. I am often asked, "Which fly are you using?" and I never like to say. I tied up a bunch of these, stuck them in my box and handed them out whenever the question arose. Then I started getting a few orders for them as a stillwater-trout pattern. Not being one to miss the boat, I started fishing them myself. It's worked for crappies, sunfish, mooneye, rainbow and browns. It is a good fly to use in slow clear water, or in still water when there is hardly a ripple. "Who'd have thunk it?" The mylar tinsel can be stretched in order to get the desired width for the fly. Caribou is finer than deer hair and produces a neater head. An interesting variation on this fly is one I developed for gar pike. This pattern is dressed on a 9671 in sizes 16 or 14 and is highly effective.

Tail: None
Body: Flat gold mylar
Wing: Yellow marabou, then two grizzly
hackle tips dyed yellow
Head: Spun and clipped caribou

White Zonker

Hook: Mustad 9671 sizes 2 to 12
Wing: A white rabbit strip
Body: Small-diameter silver mylar piping.
On size 8 and smaller, use flat silver
tinsel

This Zonker variation is designed for fishing bass, pike, muskie, bowfin, salmon and steelhead in clear water. The white wing is easily seen by the fish, and the silver provides flash. This combination will get the fish's attention, but it is not too gaudy to spook them in the gin-clear water. I first started fishing it in 1980 and it has become one of my "stand-by" flies. To say that I invented it would be misleading. As is so often the case, the lineage of a fly can be as checkered as a chessboard. This is my variation of the Zonker (U.S.), which is a variation of the New Zealand Maori pattern the Rabbit, which was used by the Maori as early as the 1920s. In 1932, Alan Duncum was fishing in the Waikato River and was sharing the shelter of a tree in a rain storm with a Maori angler who showed him the pattern. Perhaps this pattern should be called the Silver Rabbit. However, "silver rabbit" evokes images of Alice in Wonderland or tinfoil, a few onions and an exquisite meal. Using a White Zonker on bright midsummer days will usually take a few bass. In rivers, it is best fished down and across. In still water, it should be retrieved very, very, very slowly. The addition of a blood-red collar, before the wing is tied down, will make the pattern more appealing to species like bass, pike, muskie and bowfin. If a collar of purple or silver doctor blue is used, the fly will be more tempting to steelhead and salmon.

Winkie

Hook: 9671 sizes 4 or 6
Body: Small-diameter silver mylar piping
Underwing: White calf tail

Midwing: Kelly green Krystal flash
Overwing: Black Krystal flash
Eyes: Yellow dot of head cement
Pupil: Black dot of head cement

I developed this pattern in 1981 as a copy of the Rapala body-bait type of lures. It is a good pattern for "chucking off" the breakwall at places like Owen Sound, Bronte Creek, Meaford and Port Elgin. When the steelhead are further up the river, the fly should be tied down to a size 8. It is a good idea to check out the size of the local minnows and match the size of your winkie to the size of the bait fish. Quite often anglers throw out minnow patterns by looking at the water conditions and not at the size of the prey there are imitating. I use the small size mylar so that the flash from the fly will not spook fish in clear water. It will catch salmon, splake, browns and steelhead. Some anglers are using winkies for smallmouth bass.

The fly was named when I was babysitting and some of my fishing buddies were over tying up batches of those "minnowy things" for the upcoming steelhead season. The fresh diaper was almost secured in place – locked and loaded – and we we're playing the "Hi, Winkie, Bye, Winkie" game. Open diaper, "Hi, winkie," ... gurgle, chuckle, smile ... Close diaper, "Bye, Winkie!" ... big smile, gurgle, gurgle chuckle. From the kitchen table came the suggestion, "Why don't you call these Winkies? Think of the fun we can have with it." So we did. To cover our tracks, we started a rumor that the fly got its name from the way it "twinkles" in the water. I still get a laugh when someone is mouthing off in a tackle shop, saying, "Oh, yeah, my girlfriend uses big Winkies." Maybe that's why she's had that unsatisfied look since she started dating you, buddy. Then there is the classic from a guy up to his armpits in ice and slush wading for steelhead: "My small blue Winkie is working great!" It leaves you thinking, "If I had a small blue winkie, I wouldn't be bragging about it and I'd be contacting someone in the medical profession." You've obviously been out there too long, my friend. Other good fish-catching color variations are:

Body	Calf tail	Midwing	Overwing
silver	white	pink	pearl
silver	black	purple	kelly green
silver	white	purple	black
gold	gray	bronze	black
gold	yellow	black	kelly green

Zulu

Hook: 3399 sizes 6 to 14

Tail: Tuft of red wool

Body: Black seal's fur

Rib: Oval or flat silver tinsel

Hackle: Palmered black

This fly is very popular in the U.K. but is seldom fished on this side of the pond, which is a pity, for it catches lots of fish. It will catch speckles, browns, rainbows, bass, perch, carp and mooneye. Sizes 6 and 8 are excellent when night fishing for steelhead or salmon. Tradition has it that the fly's name was inspired by the headdresses of the Zulu warriors from the Boer War.

Acknowledgments

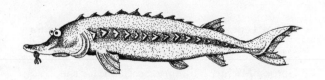

Lots of folk did lots of things to get this book to press, and for that I am extremely grateful. You know what you did and I do, too. From the experts on both sides of the Atlantic who advised on the technical stuff, through to all those pressed into manuscript duty, my warmest and deepest thanks, especially:

Professor Jack Alex, Guelph, for all things botanical

The Big Brancher, thanks is not enough; may the pipes play the "Flowers of the Forest"

Carley, Kim and Paul at Mad Mallard Graphics, "Let's do lunch or bagels"

Cathy at Mabel's Fables, Toronto, for the manuscript's first steps

Dr. Boris Chambule, Toronto, for all things chiropractic

The Dead Dog Cafe, Blossom, Alberta, "Great laughs and great coffee"

Dick, the English Critic

David Hall and Basil Shields, County Mayo, Ireland, for the information on the Irish flies

Hugo, champion of the Mac 7.5.3 operating system and the scuzzi lock out

Jan, for keeping me near the path, and mukwa for insight; *chi miigwetch*

Jan, the English Critic's critic

Ginty Jocius, Guelph, "New York, New York ... and Vilnius! *Aciu labai.*"

Joan Kirkham, one of Canada's best tiers and an inspiration to all who own a vise

Cliff Lax, Toronto, for looking at—and understanding—the legal bits

John and Geraldine McConnell, Adrigole, Ireland, for help with the illustrations

The McLennans: Ann, Ben, Lauren and Willie for the laughs, help and hand-made boxer shorts

Gordon Michie, Ballingry, Scotland, for the information on the U.K. flies

Brian Reynolds, you read the first stuff and I hope you're still laughing

John Roberts, Clifton, England, for the information on the other U.K. flies

Shelley, David and Ron at Reel Drag Productions, "Get out the 52 Buick"

Stephan, "Here we go! Disregard." It's another great day for a Loogan Fest

Thumper the Wool Baroness, a never-ending source of 100% pure and all-natural tying materials

Robert Wade, New York, for comparing notes on how to teach "into-the-wind casting techniques"

Wigwam Digital Ltd., Scotland, for all the solid ideas, counsel and comments

All the staff at HarperCollins, in particular:

Don, the best editor I have ever had, "Just a few more wee details!"

Evan, for the fantastic job on the endpapers

Jessica, thanks for your editorial diligence and taking your work home

Neil, thanks for all the production-related bits and pieces

Nicole, thank God for another Aquarian

Norma, the queen of the phone and the front desk

Roy, for your amazing hard work and for catching the ones the other folks missed

Inspirational music was provided by AC/DC, Beethoven, Blue Oyster Cult, Deana Carter, The Corries, Deacon Blue, The Dubliners, Fred J. Eaglesmith and the Flying Squirrels, The Fureys, Goodbye Mr. McKenzie, Grieg, Hipsway, Hue and Cry, The Sensational Alex Harvey Band, Leahey, Don McLean, Ralph McTell, Mozart, Red Ellis, Stan Rogers, Texas, The Who, Queen and Zero Zero.

Note: Fly fishermen should be like magicians ... never show your hand. As you should have expected, many names have been changed to protect the guilty. To avoid excessive angling pressure on stocks of wild fish like carp, bowfin, sheephead, redhorse and gar pike—and to preserve the unspoiled beauty of environmentally sensitive areas and heavy industrial outflows—I have also switched some locations. Please keep in mind the Great Auk, or look at the cod stock levels, and practice catch and release.

"I'd never join any club that would have me as a member." Groucho Marx.

Illustrations

The paper used for the drawings was 80 lb 400 Series, Strathmore Drawing premium recycled. The Plonker, Mugwump, pheasant tail feather and mallard duck flank feather were illustrated using a Gillott 1950 nib and black Koh-I-Noor universal India ink. All other drawings were done with technical pens using size 0.18mm and 0.13mm points. All illustrations: Ian Colin James.

Index of Fly Patterns

Notes

Notes

Notes

Notes

Notes

Notes

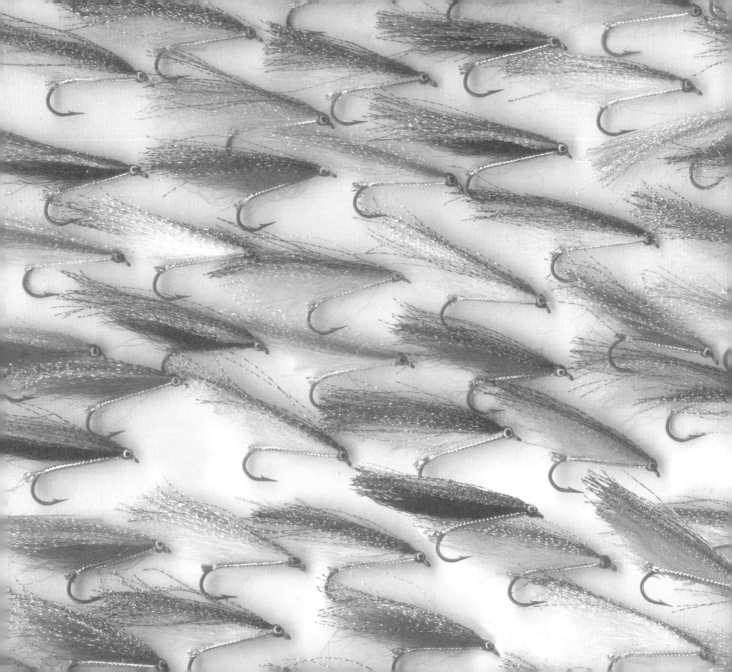